IRISH
TWEED

'Pure wool Irish tweed is a sensual creation;

it appeals to our tactile urges.'

Vawn Corrigan

Vawn Corrigan's first book, *Irish Aran: History, Tradition, Fashion* (2019), was published by The O'Brien Press as part of their O'Brien Irish Heritage series, and her writings on Irish craft have appeared in the *Irish Arts Review*, *Irish Antiques Journal*, *Ireland of the Welcomes* and the international textiles magazine *Selvedge*. Vawn lives in Dublin and enjoys collaborations exploring heritage and living craft traditions.

Reviews of Irish Aran: History, Tradition, Fashion

'a popular history that explains what made Aran so special and how its legacy is continually refreshed and modernised' Deirdre McQuillan, fashion editor, *Irish Times* in the *Irish Arts Review*

'a fascinating read' *RTÉ Guide*

'fabulous book' RTÉ TV's *Today Show*

'a must for anyone interested in Irish fashion' *Dubray Books*

IRISH
TWEED
HISTORY
TRADITION
FASHION

VAWN CORRIGAN

THE O'BRIEN PRESS
DUBLIN

Dedication

For Tom Canning

First published 2020 by
The O'Brien Press Ltd,
12 Terenure Road East, Rathgar, D06 HD27, Dublin 6, Ireland.
Tel: +353 1 4923333; Fax: +353 1 4922777
E-mail: books@obrien.ie
Website: www.obrien.ie
The O'Brien Press is a member of Publishing Ireland.

ISBN: 978-1-78849-021-4

9 8 7 6 5 4 3 2 1
24 23 22 21 20

Book cover main image: photograph by Vawn Corrigan, jacket courtesy of Sinéad Kane.
Bottom image on back cover: courtesy of Foxford Woollen Mills.

Printed and bound in Poland by Białostockie Zakłady Graficzne S.A.
The paper in this book is produced using pulp from managed forests.

Published in

CONTENTS

A LONG TRADITION

'To be human is to be involved with cloth.'

Beverly Gordon, *Textiles: The Whole Story*

Weaving is perhaps the most ancient craft of all; ever since early humans began interlacing branches for shelters to rest within and containers to carry food, we have been weaving. Sophistication in weaving is often taken as an indicator of a stable society since it takes free time and an ample supply of food to develop this basic craft into a weaving tradition. Until the days of mass production of textiles, cloth generally held a high place in global culture. Many countries around the world still produce their own distinctive textiles which hold a particular place in nations' hearts. For hundreds of years, Ghana's weavers have been making Kente, and for Ghanaians the colours in their distinctive silk and cotton fabric carry specific meanings. Japan has Yuzen silk, a cut velvet cloth usually reserved for kimonos, which has associations with emperors of the past. For Ireland, tweed communicates our story.

Weaving reached a very high standard in Ireland centuries ago. Cloth once served as currency to be exchanged for goods, or as a tribute to the High Kings and Queens of ancient Ireland. Ireland enjoys a year-round temperate and damp climate which results in superb pastures for agriculture. Traditionally, creating textiles went hand-in-hand with farming. Ireland's first farmers began cultivating crops and growing flax for weaving linen around six thousand years ago. Early sheep were hairy and their fleece was relatively useless for creating yarn. The first woolly sheep were bred in ancient Mesopotamia (modern-day Iraq) around four thousand years ago. Shortly afterwards, they arrived in Ireland and weaving with wool began. It never stopped. Though linen has a longer history in the country, it was wool that met the primary clothing needs of the Irish for centuries.

Although we have found countless objects which help to date our weaving tradition, textile archaeologists are hampered by the scarcity

Tweeds from Magee 1866 (left) and the unspoilt landscape close to their woollen mill in Donegal town (above). Traditionally, the artistry of Donegal tweed reflects its primary source of inspiration – the natural beauty surrounding the makers.

of cloth for study because textiles are so fragile and wool degrades very rapidly in alkaline conditions. A collection of items was recovered from the bogs of County Antrim in the early 1900s. Among them was a fragment of ancient plain weaving known as the Armoy cloth after the place in which it was found. Dating from about the eighth century BC, it is the oldest surviving cloth found in the country so far. But we know that weaving is much older than this fragment. The find shows that a form of heddle, the part which separates the warp yarn to allow the weaver to make patterns, was already in use.

Tweed is part of a larger culture of making that was core to Irish life for centuries. The early Irish textile industry was once well developed and spread across the country; it included raw materials such as flax and wool. The yarns were spun from them and from imported fibres such as cotton and silk. All manner of things were brought to a high standard to provide functional and luxury goods for home and abroad. Everything from marquees and tents for armies, to uniforms, sails, ropes and nets for boats were all exported from Ireland. Garments and accessories of every description – woollen cloaks, linen shirts, silk poplin ball gowns, hosiery and millinery – were all manufactured in the country. Entire areas formed a network of textile workshops and small factories, in which generations were employed. To say that Ireland has had a profound relationship with textiles is an understatement; it is part of who we are.

Visitors to the Liberties area of Dublin may notice street signs such as Weaver's Square and repurposed old buildings such as the Tenterhouse. The area was once a major textile hub. These vestiges are all that remain of the several hundred small textile factories and workshops that were in the area up until the mid-1950s. In the eighteenth century, whatever you needed for each stage of life – from christening gowns to wedding hats, from the mattress you slept on to the silk lining for your coffin – was all made in the Liberties. The history goes back even further than this.

The Liberties area was associated with weaving before the Vikings' arrival in Ireland, around 841. When excavation took place in nearby Dublin's Wood Quay, the richness of the weaving culture of Viking Dublin was revealed by all manner of weaving equipment such as spindle whorls (for spinning) and beaters and combs, many of which

One of the team of hand weavers in Studio Donegal, County Donegal, handweaving Donegal Tweed from pure wool yarn spun in their own mill.

were carved from bone and inscribed with runic script. Even now, digging foundations for buildings in the city can turn up a wealth of pieces related to weaving, dating back over a thousand years.

A trip around the country will reveal similar stories elsewhere. As the west of Ireland was the last sight of land for ships to the United States, it was where they stocked up on what was required for the journey. Cork's textile industry also developed in part because of this strong trade in the fine, wide harbour of Cobh. Aside from functional weaving, on the luxury end, Irish silk poplin, handmade lace, and linen were of such quality that their market included the royal courts of Europe and the wealthiest people in the world.

In nineteenth-century Limerick, the production of lace was on an industrial scale, and the county had one of the first assembly-line factories in the world – Taits clothing factory, the world's largest clothing supplier.

Until the late 1960s, the number of people who were employed in the textile industry was as high as twenty-five percent of the work-force. The days of manufacturing are largely over. What remains is a small group of makers who operate outside the mainstream. Their cloth is an artisan product, valued for its superb quality.

The history of making tweed provides an attractive backstory and great design continues to carry it. The level of expertise behind Ireland's sustainable production and the use of natural fibres are also integral parts of the appeal of Irish tweed.

Donegal Tweed is one of the world's most prestigious textiles and a rare survivor of the country's venerable lineage of textiles. Though significantly less renowned than our musical and literary tradition, our native textiles are part of who we are as a people. Irish tweed tells the story of the island of Ireland itself.

Chapter One

A FEEL FOR TWEED

'Pure wool Irish tweed is a sensual creation;

it appeals to our tactile urges.'

Vawn Corrigan

Tweed is an adaptable fabric that offers warmth, insulation and a degree of weatherproofing. It is a relatively loose weave, beloved by designers for its drape, and by those who wear it for its ability to mould itself to the body without losing its shape. As a natural woollen textile, it has a breathable quality. Before the advent of high-performance fabrics such as Gore-Tex, it was considered optimum for outdoor wear for activities such as mountaineering, horse riding and golfing.

Today we have numerous choices of fabrics. Our lifestyles have changed; we have public transport, cars and central heating. Irish tweed has got softer and lighter in response. The sorts of yarns, or threads, used in weaving have changed. While once it was most associated with outdoor clothing, its uses have expanded greatly. Stout and heavier tweeds are in demand, particularly for headwear, bags, coats and waistcoats, but the range is such that a designer may choose Irish tweed for even the lightest evening dress. It remains a casual cloth, unlike the sleek worsted wool fabrics you might recognise in formal suits. It has also become a firm favourite in homeware design, where it is prized for its durability and the wonderful textures it offers. The reason we choose tweed is primarily for the aesthetic. While some weaving is all about complexity, tweed has a kind of honest, simple appeal. Colour and texture are its two supreme features.

TWEED'S ORIGINS

The word 'tweed' is generally defined in dictionaries as a coarse woollen cloth handwoven along the western seaboard of Ireland, England and Scotland. Irish tweed has outgrown this definition; it is no longer coarse or necessarily handwoven.

There is some confusion about the origin of the word. There is a river Tweed on the border between Scotland and England, which historically was the location for many textile mills; thus it was suggested that the cloth had been named after the river. However, it is generally agreed that the word came into use when an English clerk mistakenly recorded 'tweel' as 'tweed' in 1826. Tweel is the Scottish word for twill, a simple weaving pattern in common usage for several hundreds of years in Ireland and Scotland before this time.

Despite similarities between the weaving traditions, Irish tweed is not of Scottish origin. It has had its own distinct and ancient path.

HOMESPUN AND TWEED

Homespun is the forerunner of our modern tweed. The name gives the clue to its manufacture; the entire sequence which moved the wool from local sheep onto people's bodies was carried out as a domestic craft. Making homespun cloth was so labour-intensive that people did not have extensive wardrobes as they currently do. In nineteenth-century Ireland, it would have been usual for many to have just two sets of clothing: one for everyday wear and one for 'Sunday best'.

Richly textured pure wool tweeds created by Magee 1866.

Girls' skirts were made with folds to be let down as they grew, the seats of men's trousers were looser for working and everyone's clothes were patched to ensure that they lasted as long as possible. Irish people's everyday clothing was made from homespun cloth for centuries. It was so ubiquitous that the terms 'homespuns' and 'clothes' were interchangeable.

The primary difference between homespuns and contemporary tweed lies in the yarns used to weave the cloth. In wool terms, the word 'handle' refers to the feel of the wool. The year-round damp in Ireland means that the breeds of sheep which thrive best produce coarse handle fleece more suited to household insulation or carpets than wearable garments. Homespun was a rough fabric made from this fleece. The practice of bringing other breeds from different countries and importing softer handle wools to combine with local wool has been ongoing for well over a hundred years. Contemporary Irish garment tweed is softer than homespun and early tweed. The texture may come as a surprise; there is nothing scratchy or stiff about it. It has a delicious yielding quality. The feel of one hundred percent Irish tweed cannot be replicated by artificial fibres.

THE RAW MATERIAL

Every metre of tweed begins with a sheep grazing on a field or hillside. Once sheared, their fleece is the natural, versatile raw material for weaving. The sorts of fleeces we use have changed over time in an effort to get a softer handle. To get the right balance of softness and structure lambswool may be combined with adult wool from various

Men from Bonmahon Copper Mines in Waterford showing woollen textiles and caps in everyday menswear at the start of the twentieth century.

Working with pure Irish wool at Cushendale Woollen Mills, in County Kilkenny.

sheep breeds. When fleeces from different sheep are combined it is termed crossbred wools. This is the most common sort of yarn used in today's Irish tweed. When you see 'Irish wool' on a label it may refer to Irish-*spun* wool, rather than wool of one hundred percent Irish origin. Irish wool continues to be important in tweed; it has the character that softer wools, such as merinos, lack. Although the prices that it fetches do not incentivise its production, there is a resurgence of interest in the traceability and provenance of wool, which has led to a rise in interest in Irish wools, as will be seen later.

CARDING AND SPINNING YARNS

While technology has altered over the years, the essential steps which go into making a woollen yarn for weaving tweed remain unchanged. Bales of one hundred percent natural raw wool are taken in and the wool is opened and scoured. Scouring means cleaning and preparing. After this it may be dyed, washed and dried, and oiled before teasing to open out the fibres. The wool is then *carded* to align the fibres and ready it for spinning. Carding is rather like brushing hair; the addition of oil stops the wool from snapping. After carding the wool is so light and soft it most resembles strings of candyfloss.

Carding readies the fleece for spinning. Archaeological digs show that spinning yarns using drop spindles predates the use of the spinning wheel. Once their use was established, spinning wheels scarcely changed through the centuries.

In Ireland, spinning was usually women's work within the home.

Before machinery, carding was done by hand using two paddles rather like flat hairbrushes. To ease the tedium, sometimes there were 'carding parties' where people would card together while chatting and singing songs.

DONEGAL COTTAGE INDUSTRIES. CARDING AND SPINNING. 9174. W.L.

When there were large families to clothe, the spinning wheels were seldom still. Consequently, the image of women at their spinning wheels became something of a romantic symbol of Ireland in the nineteenth century.

A machine for spinning with more than one spindle at a time, known as the Spinning Jenny, came to Ireland in the eighteenth century. Machine spun (millspun) yarns have a more even tension and are less likely to snap when weaving. The attendant costs of transporting wool to mills put it out of the reach of many rural people who practised weaving as a domestic craft. The use of the spinning wheel for creating tweed had largely been abandoned by the middle of the twentieth century. Once millspun yarns were used, the term homespun no longer accurately described the cloth.

Hand-carding and spinning are so time-consuming that they are now seldom done outside of the spheres of fibre art, for the creation of highly individualised small pieces, or as a heritage hobby.

Weaving yarns need to be stronger and more elastic than knitting yarns, and so are usually single-ply (single strand), while knitting yarn is two-ply (double strand). The techniques used to create yarn for weaving will create very different results.

Typically, uniforms and classic formalwear suits are made of *worsted* wool fabric; if you run your hand over worsted fabrics you will find them slick to the touch. This is because the yarns for worsteds are combed so that the fleece fibres all run in the same direction. In most European countries 'worsted' yarn is known as 'combed' yarn.

In contrast, for Irish tweed yarns, some of the wool fibres are

BARNEY'S BLARNEY.

Irish women at their spinning wheels was once such a common sight that there are countless such depictions to be found in vintage illustrations and postcards. The long strands of flax on the distaff of the wheel tell us that the woman is spinning linen yarn. The title 'Barney's Blarney' refers to the belief that kissing the Blarney stone in Cork conveyed the ability to charm with words, the 'gift of the gab'.

arranged in a random orientation. This technique also traps in more air, giving tweed great insulating properties without being heavy. Irish tweed is, therefore, not a smooth, flat fabric.

WARPING AND WEAVING

The two basic components of any sort of weaving, from rustic basketry to the finest silk, are known as the warp and the weft. Irrespective of whether the weaver uses a hand loom or a machine, every weaving project from the plainest to the most elaborate begins the same way.

The yarns which will remain stationary are fastened lengthways; this is known as 'warping the loom'. The warp must be stable and

This spinning mule from the early 1900s in Cushendale Woollen Mills is the oldest of only three spinning mules still in operation in Ireland. Philip Cushen (pictured here) from the mill explains: 'Using a spinning mule creates a semi-worsted feel to the yarn so that it most closely resembles the drawn fibre feel of handspun yarn.'

strong because its active partner, the weft, will be interlaced in an over-and-under sequence to create the material.

VARIOUS WEAVING PATTERNS

In the 1950s an excavation of a Passage Tomb in Fourknocks, County Meath unearthed a pottery food vessel that contained imprints of a woven cloth. Based on this discovery, we understand that the patterns that are still used in Irish tweed date back to Neolithic times (*c.*1600 BC). The patterns of Irish tweed are relatively simple, yet an almost limitless variety of cloth can be created. The way that the weaver sets up their loom and ties up their chosen yarns before they begin is what dictates the sorts of designs that can result from the dance between the active weft and the stationary warp. The weaver's choices around colour combinations and the diameter of the yarns they use in the warp and the weft expand these possibilities.

Worker at the warp in Foxford Woollen Mills, County Mayo, which was founded in 1892.

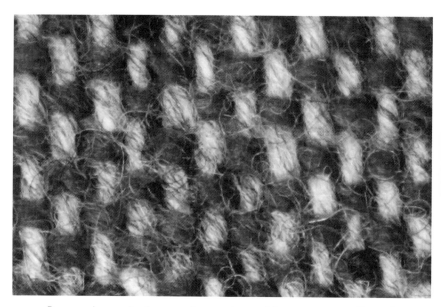

Pure wool yarns dyed, spun and woven into a plain weave pattern. Created in Kerry Woollen Mills, the eighteenth-century mill in County Kerry, for Hanna Hats, Donegal. It is known as salt 'n' pepper tweed because of the contrasting colours.

PLAIN OR TABBY WEAVE

A plain weave, which is also known as a tabby weave and a 'one and one', is the simplest of the weaving patterns. You will see it around you in cloth that is often used for shirts. It has a basic criss-cross pattern rather like a checkerboard. It is called 'one and one' because every time the weft goes over the yarn its next step is to go under. In Ireland, the use of a dark weft against a light-coloured warp is known as salt 'n' pepper tweed. This is perhaps the oldest traditional Donegal Tweed pattern. Its name derives from the fact that it was commonly created using a combination of either undyed dark wool or wool dyed dark, with undyed white wool.

TWILL

As you might guess from the fact that the word tweed derives from twill, it is the most common weave for tweed. Twill is a very popular weave for strong fabrics. You will see the twill pattern on denim and recognise it by its diagonal ribbed surface. Twill can be so subtle that the cloth seems plain unless viewed closely; if the thickness of the yarn is increased the pattern is exaggerated for a more extrovert look. Broken twill is the term used when the pattern is interrupted for variety.

Extracts from textile artist Terry Dunne's notebook on how to set up a hand loom for weaving a twill tweed pattern, known as two-by-two. Herringbone, seen on the right, is a twill variation or a broken twill pattern. It derives its name from its similarity to a fish skeleton.

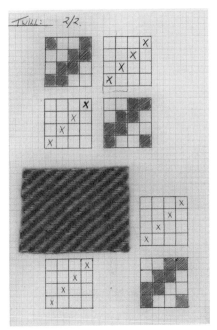

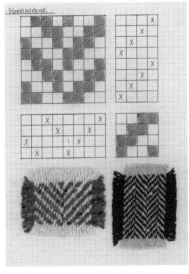

VARIATIONS

There are myriad variations on primary tweed patterns that chiefly involve changes in scale and colours. An example is the very familiar houndstooth tweed. It is a 'four and four': four yarns of light colour are followed by four yarns of dark colour so that it creates its distinctive pattern. The name derives from its similarity to a dog's tooth.

Overlaying a chequered pattern in a smaller size can make the fabric appear monochrome until viewed up close, whereas when it is scaled upwards the broad paths of intersecting colour create visual fields of surprise. Plaid is the word used to describe checks and these can be used so sparsely that they simply introduce thin intersecting lines of colour, or densely so that the fabric is full of cubes of different colour. Window-pane patterns, like the name implies, are frames of colour which often contain a more neutral base colour.

FINISHING

Irish tweed's ability to keep its shape is due to expert finishing, which 'sets' the fabric. During the finishing process, the fabric is carefully pre-shrunk to stabilise it and to achieve the desired thickness. From the thirteenth century, local mills (known as fulling mills) offered finishing using a simple water-powered box container with large wooden blocks that pummelled the wet cloth. This replaced the exhausting work of kicking the wet fabric to-and-fro (usually men's work), known as 'waulking'. Today, this first phase of finishing the tweed is called wet-finishing, and it takes place in machines resembling giant washing machines.

Right: Hanna Hats' tweed cap, featuring herringbone tweed from Kerry Woollen Mills. Below: Foxford Woollen Mills' pure wool wrap in a classic black-and-white houndstooth tweed, coupled with a tweed handbag featuring a smaller houndstooth, woven in a check pattern.

Here, a pure wool Irish tweed from Avoca weaving mill, County Wicklow, features a combination of a herringbone pattern with a bold over-pattern of broad checks.

Handwoven vintage tweed from The Weavers Shed, Kilmainham, Dublin.
The image on the left shows the tweed before milling.

In some tweeds you may notice a degree of felting of the surface; this is from milling, an extended wet-finishing process, in which a controlled amount of friction is applied to the surface of the cloth when it is wet. Milling makes the fabric more weatherproof and more stable for harder wear.

Originally, damp homespun would have been rolled up tightly so that it kept its shape to some degree. Now, the dry-finishing processes include the application of heat in controlled conditions, such as a purpose-made dry room. Permanent pleats remain in a fabric unless it is subjected to a greater temperature than that which was used to set them; the same principle applies to tweeds; they too will keep their shape unless exposed to higher temperatures than those used in the

Tweed has a natural fuzzy surface, although this can be smoothed by shaving, or cropping, during the dry-finishing process if a smoother look is desired.

finishing process. 'Raising' is a process that brushes the surface of the tweed to encourage the natural fleecy softness of the fibres. The number of times this is done dictates how fluffy the resultant fabric will be.

DONEGAL AND HARRIS TWEED

Donegal Tweed is not monochrome. It has a lustre to it, created by multiple flecks of contrasting colour, sometimes as many as ten different colours, against a base tone. This lively colour effect has been described as viewing the landscape through mist. The little points of colour may resemble wildflowers set against dark bogland or glimpses of heather over cloudy mountainscapes, such as in the landscape pictured right.

DONEGAL TWEED

Donegal Tweed takes its name from the place where it originated; the dramatically beautiful region in the northwest of the country. This region has had a strong weaving tradition for hundreds of years and Donegal remains the heartland of our national cloth.

Originally, when tweed yarns were produced by hand, little wads of wool would ball up and these little burrs would resist the base colour dye or take it differently, resulting in a flecked appearance. The mark of homespun tweed was this flecked look and it gave the fabric

interest. Today, this effect is widely emulated. It is created by feeding in differently coloured burrs of wool during the carding process.

HARRIS TWEED

Donegal Tweed shares the world stage alongside another famous tweed, Harris Tweed from Scotland. *Clò-Mòr*, the original Gaelic term for the tweed, was first referred to as Harris Tweed in 1840 when the Countess of Dunmore recognised the potential of the cottage industry to uplift the fishing communities of the Hebridean islands. In this regard it has a parallel with Irish tweed as will be seen later. Harris Tweed is protected by a trademark which stipulates that every process must take place on the island (carding, spinning, dyeing, weaving and finishing). It is handwoven, and the looms are powered by foot pedals rather like on bicycles. The advantage of a trademark is that the islanders have been able to hold on to their industry. By building the brand of Harris Tweed, and having government support and protection for it, four hundred islanders in the trade can rely on it for their livelihoods.

In contrast, Donegal Tweed has become a generic term describing tweeds with flecks of colour. It may be termed Donegal Tweed even if it is made elsewhere. The Italians produce world-class textiles

A suit from Kevin & Howlin, Dublin, made using Donegal Tweed woven in Donegal from pure wool spun in Donegal Yarns. Opposite: The bale of pure wool in Donegal Yarns shows the differently dyed pure wool.

and many Italian mills produce 'Donegals', as do German and Portuguese mills. It is a compliment, but it is also frustrating. For the Irish tweed enthusiasts these imitations are easily spotted. They are have been described as flatter and duller than the real thing. The expertise and processes are not the same and real Donegal Tweed remains a superior product.

Lorna Macaulay, Chief Executive of the Harris Tweed Authority, observes the differences between the Harris Tweed industry and the Donegal Tweed industry:

'Ireland does craft so well. I recognise that in relation to Irish tweed your government bodies haven't yet taken the steps of protection that we have; we get enormous support to protect Harris Tweed, but I do feel that there is a real pride in Ireland.'

The question of protecting Donegal Tweed with a trademark has been circulating for a long time. The Design and Crafts Council of Ireland (DCCoI) is currently working with Mairéad McGuinness, Vice President of the European Parliament, to get the same protection for Donegal Tweed that other regional products enjoy. This has already happened with food products, for example the Waterford *blaa*, the white bread roll associated with County Waterford. There is a downside to trademarking Donegal Tweed: the concept of authenticity, which implies something with fixed and demonstrable qualities, can be somewhat confining. Irish tweed makers are hopeful of establishing their ownership of the name Donegal Tweed while still enjoying a degree of flexibility about which yarns are used and whether the tweeds are handwoven or power-loomed.

IRISH TWEED – HANDWOVEN OR POWER-LOOMED?

Creating textiles has always been hard physical work, which is why it was mechanised so early. Machines have been in use in Ireland from the late 1800s. These early power looms usually had cast-iron components and were driven using belts and pulleys turned using the energy from rivers harnessed by mill races. Diesel engines followed

One of the mill team in Foxford Woollen Mills working on the creel of the warping machine, picking up a broken warp thread and making a weaver's knot. Warping on a power loom, the procedure which precedes every weaving project can take as long as two days.

and sometimes worked in tandem with hydropower up until Irish rural electrification began in 1949. Today the vast majority of Irish tweed is power-loomed. Sophisticated and costly machines are driven by electricity and green energy. The misconception that power-looming textiles is as easy as flicking a switch and out pops fabric is quickly corrected on a mill tour. The machines are complex and using them requires a great deal of training and specialist knowledge.

Despite the availability of machinery, hand weaving maintained a central role in the story of Irish textiles. In Europe, weaving skills had largely moved out of the home entirely by the late 1800s. But in Ireland the existing domestic tradition was developed further into a strong home industry for regions with poor land and high unemployment from this period onwards. Hand weaving continued to be supported right up until the late 1960s. The majority of the country's hand weavers are based in Donegal, the region where tweed was brought to its zenith in the nineteenth century, and where it has continued in unbroken line through the generations.

Handwoven tweed may still be purchased in Ireland, both by the metre and made up into garments and accessories. It is labour-intensive, skilled work and the price reflects this. Those who choose handwoven tweed are happy to pay the premium for it; the backstory of the tradition is as much part of the appeal as the look and feel of the cloth.

The two disciplines are not in competition. They operate in entirely different spheres in terms of the volume they can produce, their cost and their market. Small runs of unique cloth are a speciality of hand weavers. The artistic character that hand weavers can put into their cloth elevates it above power-loomed cloth aesthetically.

BÁINÍN

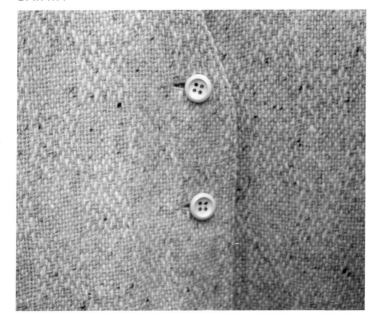

While Irish tweed is appreciated for its fine use of colour, and particularly for its ability to capture the rich hues of the natural world, not all tweed involves the use of colour. Báinín is a traditional Irish tweed created using undyed white wool. The word derives from bán (white). This sort of cloth was so commonly used to make up men's waistcoats, particularly around the west coast of the country, that the garment itself became known as báinín. It has featured in Irish fashion design throughout the decades and today it is used by some of the country's top designers.

Chapter Two

SAINTS AND REBELS

'Entitled is the great king of the Feara Manach to five cloaks with

golden borders, five shields, five swords of battle,

five ships, five coats of mail [armour]'

Extract from the medieval text *The Book of Rights*

Unlike the Romans, Irish culture was not written; instead, centuries of Irish life were preserved orally in sagas, stories and poems. From the fourth century onward, the remains of this cultural heritage were transcribed. Old Irish differs somewhat from modern Irish, known as *Gaeilge*. We rely on a combination of the Old Irish, Latin transcriptions of the oral tradition, the illustrations in the Book of Kells (circa ninth century), and early Christian stone carvings to help piece together a picture of what the ancient Irish wore. From studying these sources, as well as Icelandic and European accounts, we know that for centuries one of the most common outfits for the Irish of both sexes was a variety of linen tunics or smocks known as *léine*, worn under a woollen cloak or mantle, known as a *brat*.

Léine were commonly made from Irish linen and gathered up by belts from which weapons and purses hung. Early Christian stone carvings suggest they were often embroidered at the hem and breast. Léine are described as saffron in colour, a dye which comes from the crocus flower stamen, though it is likely that the bright yellow colour was also achieved using the oldest and most commonly used dyestuff *crottle*, from the Irish word *crotal*, which is a lichen found on rocks.

Our ancient Irish peers wore voluminous shaggy brats. They were truly a multipurpose item: clothes by day and blankets by night. Whether you were a queen or a slave, wore silk or rags, you were most likely clad in a brat. Colourful patterned borders were woven to trim them. It's most likely that the body of brats were monochrome; the surface of the woollen cloth was curled or loops were woven into the weft. This trapped more air, making the fabric resistant to the elements and very warm. Inside the brat a microclimate protected the wearer. It seems to have been very effective as there are many accounts of people sleeping outdoors enveloped by their brats.

Hand-weaving instructor and textile researcher Annie Dibble was tasked by the Office of Public Works to create historically accurate clothing for museum purposes. Using a combination of historical sources, she designed and created a replica of an ancient Irish brat. It was based on a fragment of an Irish brat that had travelled to Brussels, where it had been venerated as a relic of the popular sixth-century saint Brigid. The ancient Celtic goddess Brigid was and still is celebrated at the Imbolc festival to mark the beginning of spring. Rather than

Replica of an ancient Irish brat based on St Brigid's Mantle, created by Annie Dibble. Annie used wool from the Jacob sheep, spun, carded and woven by hand, and the fabric was finished as in the past. Everyone was astonished at how elegant and warm it was.

being abandoned when Christianity gained dominance, the goddess was simply incorporated into early Christian lore. St Brigid's miracle story shows her connection with textiles: she wanted to set up a monastery and approached the King of Leinster, but he refused her, so she asked could she have whatever land her cloak might cover and he agreed. When she laid down her cloak it spread magically covering acres of fertile land known as St Brigid's Pastures (the Curragh, Kildare).

For centuries weaving was a commonplace domestic chore done by women. Its importance was recognised by the ancient Brehon laws, written c.AD 600–800. These remarkably enlightened codes included that in the case of divorce women were entitled to keep their weaving equipment and a share of their spun yarns and woven cloths.

Weaving skills ensured women's ability to provide.

Tweed links in to aspects of Irish culture such as the St Brigid's Cross (right). An example is seen above with the pattern on this tweed created by Magee. On St Brigid's feast day, the first day of February, it is still customary in many parts of the country to make a cross using green rushes. St Brigid's Cross is believed to protect homes from hardship.

The term spinster, now an outdated derogatory term for an unmarried woman, related to the fact that women customarily wove household linens for their family before marriage.

PASSION FOR COLOUR AND ORNAMENTATION

The sheer volume of colours mentioned in the ancient texts indicates that dyeing expertise was well-developed in ancient Ireland. As well as the use of lichen for shades of yellow, the ingredients for dyes included various seaweeds and sea life, and, from the surrounding landscape, myrtle, gorse, sloe, alder twigs, weld, foxgloves and horsetail (to name just a few). The root of the madder flower was used to create a shade ranging from orange to deep red which ultimately became connected with the traditional red tweed skirts of women in the west of the country. These continued to be worn on the Aran Islands and in parts of Connemara up until the 1950s.

Natural dyeing expertise was often the domain of female herbal healers, who knew the plants in the region well. Iron dye pots and alum, a mineral mordant (dye fixing agent) were also known in ancient Ireland.

The beautiful race of demi-gods called the *Tuatha dé Danann* dominated Irish imagination for centuries. Their adventures, combined with historic accounts of the real-life Gaelic aristocracy, make a lively read full of adventure, lust and magic. Among descriptions of heroism, feasting and love intrigues are many insights into their relationship with clothes. Tara, in County Meath was the heartland and spiritual centre of old Irish culture for centuries; the royal court

In the areas where lichen was commonly used for dyeing fabric the children were sent to scrape the lichens off the rocks in the summer months. Natural dyeing expertise is kept alive by weavers such as Beth Moran of Clare Island, whose lichen dye pot is shown here.

of Tara was home to the High Kings of Ireland, such as Cormac Mac Airt. The old texts tell that Mac Airt's daughters wove silver and gold threads into clothing. This shows that weaving was an essential part of domestic life for even the highest-ranking families. It also gives us some idea of just how luxurious the clothes of the Gaelic aristocracy must have been – brilliantly dyed and glittering with silvers and golds. In tales of the *Tuatha dé Danann* this lush description of Étain, when first seen by Eochaid Feidlech, High King of Ireland (48–44 BC) gives a taste of the sheer pleasure that was taken in colour:

'A beautiful purple cloak she had, and silver fringes to it, and a gold brooch; and she had on her a dress of green silk with a long hood, embroidered in red gold, and wonderful clasps of gold and silver on her breasts and on her shoulder. The sunlight was falling on her, so that the gold and green were shining out.'

From *Gods and Fighting Men*, Lady Gregory, 1905

Opposite: The Gaelic aristocracy may have worn brightly dyed clothing embroidered with gold and silver thread in styles like those depicted by Jim Fitzpatrick, the acclaimed Irish artist who draws from the country's Celtic lore and design for inspiration.

BREAS ASUS CÚ BREA
SAIOEAÐ: 79

BREAS AND CÚ BREA
JIM FITZPATRICK

Chapter Three

LAND OF WOOL

'As I went a walking one morning in June,

To view the fair fields and the valleys in bloom,

I spied a pretty fair maid she appeared like a queen

With her costly fine robes and her mantle so green.'

Irish song 'A Brat Chomh Deas Glas' ('Her Mantle So Green')

Empires were built on the wool trade. It was a great source of wealth, but production had to be organised for the country to benefit from it. Changes in Irish society from the twelfth century onwards saw woollen textile manufacture moving out of the domestic sphere and into organised workshops. It grew into a trans-European export trade. The Norman French invaders settled in Ireland from 1169 and shared power with the ancient Gaelic order. They were ultimately integrated and became 'more Irish than the Irish themselves'. Many changes to Irish society came from Norman influence. The Normans designed and built important walled towns and castles, and introduced

MILL RACE, MILLSTREET, CO. CORK. 7961. W.L.

Mills were often multipurpose; flour, metalwork, soap and paper production took place alongside textile processes. Small mills like this one in Millstreet, County Cork were once in virtually every village with a river.

a more organised system of labour, including urban workshops. The first record of an Irish mill dates back to the third century, when a mill was constructed on the river Nith. Mills became so numerous that beside rivers both large and small throughout the country lie the buried ruins of *muileann* (mills) and vestiges of ancient trades. Under the Normans, larger mills were built that became organised workshops for textile production. The export of Irish wool and textiles grew formidable during the thirteenth century. Trade was greatly assisted by the country's wide and safe natural harbours.

By 1357, the Italian writer Fazio degli Uberti attested that the Irish textiles which were imported to the Continent had reached such a level of perfection that they were the most highly regarded of all. Just one record from the trading port of Bristol, England shows that in the three years between 1557 and 1560 some 26,556 yards (24,300 metres) of Irish frieze (a firm woollen cloth used for capes) were imported as well as quantities of 'shag mantles'. The seaport town of Waterford in the southeast became a major hub for producing cloaks during the sixteenth century. A waist-length variety of cloak, the *mantle Irlandais,* and the old-style shaggy brats were exported all over Europe. The latter were bought in great quantities for soldiers.

When the first Weavers' Guild was established in 1446 it included male and female weavers, but as weaving became more professional, it increasingly became men's work. The Guild wielded political clout right up until the nineteenth century. This verse from 1767 was written for the annual pageant at which members participated in a public procession:

'The weavers next in order proudly ride,

who with great skill the nimble shuttle guide;

Pity such art should meet such small award;

but what art nowadays does meet regard?'

Only parts of Ireland were under English control until the sixteenth and seventeenth centuries when the Tudor monarchs determined to extend their reach. Part of this effort included forcing the populace to adopt the manners, customs, language and dress of their overlords. King Henry VIII passed legislation forbidding the wearing of brats in Ireland. It may seem strange to us that a cloak could be the subject

The illustrations in John Derricke's *The Image of Irelande* (1581) provide an insight into old Irish dress as well as the power struggle within the country. This one is captioned: 'Rorie Oge, a wild kerne [Irish soldier] and a defeated rebel, in the forest with wolves for company.'

of legislation, but for the Tudors it was a powerful symbol of cultural difference. People could sleep in the woods in it, so it was reasoned that it facilitated outlaws and rebels who could lie in wait for the English. It was argued that too much could be concealed beneath the folds of a brat, from stolen goods to weapons. In addition, those who wanted to advance in society were under pressure to abandon their Irish style of dress.

English rule was fully established in Ireland after the Flight of the Earls in 1607, when the very last of the ruling Gaelic families boarded ships to the Continent from Rathmullan, County Donegal. They aimed to raise Spanish help to defeat the Tudors, but they were never to return. The little museum that commemorates this event features replicas of clothing, discovered in the mid-nineteenth century, that had lain preserved in Irish bogland undisturbed for hundreds of years.

The original Shinrone Gown which can be seen in the National Museum, Dublin.

One find in County Tipperary was that of the Shinrone Gown, a costume that dates from the late sixteenth/early seventeenth century. It is a very rare example of early Irish textiles. Costume expert Mairéad Dunlevy isolated Flemish design influences in the Shinrone Gown. The dress was designed to open at the front to accommodate changes such as pregnancy – typical of the northern European style at the time. The well-constructed tweed dress reveals a surprisingly high standard of tailoring.

THE CLOAK – IRELAND'S MOST INDIGENOUS GARMENT

Irish cloaks or mantles were generally fuller and longer than our European counterparts. While they fell out of fashion across Europe, they continued to be worn by the Irish. Cloaks are the country's most indigenous surviving ancient dress. One particular style, the Kinsale cape, was named after the place in County Cork where it was made. It was a long woollen cloak for women which featured a very full, gathered hood. It was a costly item and was frequently passed down among families. They remain popular for dramatic evening wear and weddings. Despite a brief revival in the 1970s, cloaks for men are seldom seen today except as a short cape attached to a coat. On the other hand, for women, shorter, more practical-length cloaks (capes) are strong fashion pieces that most Irish tweed companies still produce.

The Kinsale cape and the caped-coat by Cleo, Dublin,

photographed by Mike Bunn.

Chapter Four

PATRIOTIC CLOTH

"Tis I can weave woollen and linen,

The finest folk wear on their backs;

So, girls, come give over your spinnin',

And wind off your wool and your flax!'

Old Irish ballad

Prior to the late eighteenth century the standard of living was higher in Ireland than it was for much of Europe because of the excellent woollen trade. The vigorous export market gave work to tens of thousands of 'workers of wool', as they were then termed. Most rural people also produced their own wool for clothing. Wolves had been eliminated and millions of sheep grazed freely over the countryside. The strong Irish wool trade threatened English-based wool manufacturers, who pressured parliament to legislate against the Irish woollen industry. When Viscount Wentworth, Earl of Strafford, moved into Dublin Castle in 1633 to control Irish affairs, he laid out his plan:

'I am of opinion that all wisdom advises to keep this kingdom as much subordinate and dependent upon England as is possible, and holding them from the manufacture of wool (which, unless otherwise directed, I shall by all means discourage), and then enforcing them to fetch their clothing from thence [England] … How can they depart from us without nakedness and beggary [dependency]?'

By 1673, no Irish wool product could be exported, except to certain English ports, and by 1699 it was excluded from export altogether. Jonathan Swift, author of *Gulliver's Travels* and Dean of Dublin's Saint Patrick's Cathedral, described the legislation to crush the woollen industry as 'this fatal Act'. With an excess of wool and no access to legitimate markets, smuggling to the Isle of Man became well-established. The waters off the east coast of the country were astir with countless so-called 'fishing' boats. The natural inlets and harbours of the east coast, such as Rush and Skerries, were hotbeds of smuggling between the seventeenth and eighteenth centuries.

In seventeenth-century Ireland those who refused to convert to Protestantism and swear allegiance to the crown were excluded from every aspect of power.

By the eighteenth century, Catholics had been disenfranchised entirely and the government of Ireland was almost exclusively in the hands of the Protestant minority which also owned most of the land. England lifted and dropped tariffs to suit the politically powerful lobby of manufacturers based on British soil. It was generally contentious and, at times, devastating. Despite the waves of restrictions

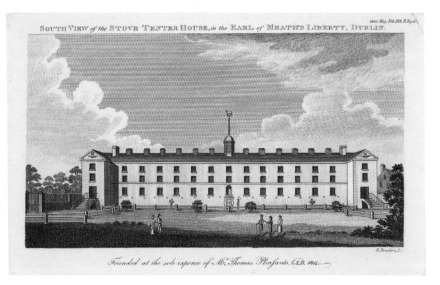

Founded at the sole expence of Mr. Thomas Pleasants. (A.D. 1814.—

The Tenterhouse (1815). The Tenters is an area in the historic textile hub of the Liberties, in Dublin. This was where fabrics were stretched out and held in place with tenterhooks, to control shrinkage during the finishing process. As it was weather-dependent, the building of the Tenterhouse was a very welcome addition. Four furnaces provided central heating within the three-storey, eighty-four-metre-long brick building.

on Irish textiles, manufacturing continued to be a significant part of the economy, proving just how vigorous it was.

IRISH SILK POPLIN

Despite the challenges caused by the lack of control over the terms of trade, the country continued to grow its international reputation for excellence in textiles. One of its best-loved exports to Europe was Irish silk poplin, an unusual innovation which consisted of a silk warp with a weft of worsted woollen yarn. The wool was hidden within the silk so that it had the structure and body of woven wool with the sleek vibrancy of silk. As a hybrid fabric it avoided the prohibitions that had been imposed against the export of woollen goods.

From 1620 onwards, up to 10,000 Huguenots arrived in waves, fleeing religious persecution in France. A high proportion of them were weavers who settled in Dublin. In the Liberties area they merged with, and elevated, the existing pool of knowledge. The silk and poplin weaving industry became so significant that in 1771 almost forty percent of the 3400 looms in operation in Dublin were dedicated to silk. It has been shown that silk weaving may go back as far as the tenth century in Ireland. It was not introduced by the Huguenots as is often suggested, but they did introduce silk damask looms and expertise. Poplin production was different to regular silk weaving. It was a specialised art, and the combination of the Huguenots' high skill set and the way they guarded tradition within their own families ultimately resulted in it becoming a Huguenot profession.

Irish silk poplin was exported in quantity to the royal courts of Europe and found a place in the wardrobes of affluent Europeans and Catholic prelates from the mid-1600s onwards. Around the mid-nineteenth century poplin was subject to a prohibitive tax that ruined the market. Although the fashion for wearing it declined, it continued to be woven in the Liberties area of Dublin right up until the middle of the twentieth century, most particularly for gowns, ties and luxury curtains. Poplin was also used patriotically for armbands during the early 1900s and for Irish military medal ribbons after the Rising in 1916.

Dublin's stunning Georgian architecture dates from the period 1740–1830, when the city was considered the second city of the British Empire. Wealthy classes had poplin hats, jackets, gowns and sashes made up in the Liberties. This painting by FJ Davis shows the finery at The State Ballroom, St Patrick's Hall, Dublin Castle, c.1845. Courtesy of Sotheby's, London.

LINEN

In contrast to poplin, weaving flax into linen was an ordinary domestic craft which had been taking place in the country since before records began. We know that as early as 1542, linen yarn was exported in quantity. Most of the linen produced would have been the darker variety, such as you might see on old sacking, rather than the fine white luxury linen that we see today. From ancient times, growing flax for linen production took place all over the country;

it peaked during the eighteenth century, continuing right up until the middle of the twentieth century, after which importing flax from the Continent became the norm.

In the seventeenth century, the English government took the decision to crush the Irish wool trade with legislation prohibiting export and to promote linen production as an alternative. The Earl of Strafford imported a higher-quality flaxseed and introduced Dutch technologies for weaving and finishing the fabric to a high enough standard for the export trade. Linen was popular, but the yarn production was far more time-consuming than preparing wool for weaving; the entire process of bleach-and-finish took several months. Setting up linen production in Ireland served two purposes: to protect the English wool industry and to take advantage of the fact that wages were lower in Ireland.

The purity of the water was cited as the reason for Irish linen's unusual brightness. It was woven as fine as tissue paper and gifted to sultans and royals the world over. In the late 1700s, Drogheda was the largest linen manufacturing town on the island. The growth of Irish linen became spectacular in the eighteenth century; from over 520,000 yards in 1705 to over 40 million yards in the 1790s. It was weather-dependent as the yarn was bleached using daylight. In the nineteenth century chlorine was discovered; this bleaching agent required copious amounts of water, so large mills were established on rivers. Production moved away from small farms and into large-scale factories. The benefits of the trade were not as widely felt as the woollen trade had been; it was centred largely in northeastern Ireland, now Northern Ireland.

Though flax is not now generally grown on the island of Ireland, the few linen weavers who remain are still held in very high regard by textile enthusiasts. These include Emblem in Wexford, McNutt of Donegal, Thomas Ferguson in County Down, and companies such as Irish Linen House, who do embroidery on linen, drawing from Ireland's traditional design language.

In the tweed story, linen is important because it set the scene for the revival of the Irish wool industry that took place in the nineteenth century. It gave Ireland a reputation for producing great luxury textiles; a brand that tweed could piggyback on even after the linen trade had long declined. Before linen moved to large-scale factories there was

Eighteenth-century illustration of a bleaching room in an Irish linen mill, showing the long fibres of flax being wrung out in the foreground.

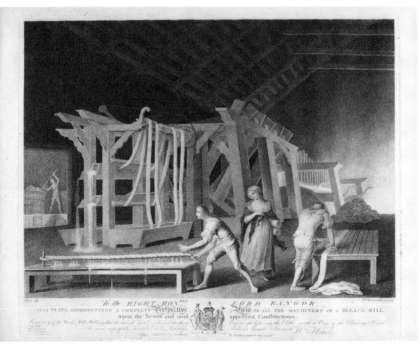

a general drive to increase production among small farming communities. Looms were supplied at cost, and in some cases for free, to incentivise production. In 1796, six thousand Saxony spinning wheels and sixty looms were given out in the Donegal region.

Flax fibres are very long, and the method of spinning yarn differs to that for wool. Aside from needing to be kept moist to release pectin in the fibre, the fibres are not simply being fed in by hand as wool is but are dressed onto an additional piece on the spinning wheel known as a distaff. Many of the original Saxony spinning wheels distributed in the eighteenth century remained in circulation and they were identifiable as such by their distaffs. No modification was required to use them for spinning wool. Similarly, eighteenth-century looms were multipurpose. The wheels and looms were copied, or repaired and kept in use over the following century. In this way, the drive for linen created the basis for the hand-weaving tradition and Donegal became a centre of domestic weaving distinction.

THE FIRST 'BUY IRISH' CAMPAIGN

In 1779, legislation against wool exporting was repealed and the trade was free again, but the large-scale woollen industry that had been developed over five centuries had been destroyed. Manufacturing textiles generally was still very important and therefore the issue of tariffs remained very contentious. When tariffs on imported goods were lifted to open the Irish market to English-based manufacturers, supporting Ireland's makers by buying Irish became a very heated political issue.

The guilds, including the Weavers' Guild, were a powerful force with political representation in the Irish parliament. They created a non-importation agreement designed to stop Irish vendors from importing English goods. Although it was not legally binding, a drive for compliance was led by the local Irish militia, the Volunteers. James Napper Tandy, later to help found the United Irishmen, was one of the leaders. Jonathan Swift added support and penned the slogan 'burn everything English but their coal'. Traders who ignored the non-importation agreement were met with looting, fires and violence. There are accounts of people being threatened and tarred and feathered for using English cloth. In one account a 'mob' of weavers caused such destruction that the army was brought in against them and one of their faction was killed.

'Ye noblemen, in place or out,

Ye Volunteers, so brave and stout,

Ye dames that flaunt at ball or rout,

Wear Irish manufacture

… Nor richest squire, nor proudest peer

Need scorn our humbler homespun gear;

No stuff on earth will wear and tear

Like Irish manufacture'

Extract from 'Irish Manufacture – a New Ballad', *c.*1779

Chapter Five

FROM DONEGAL TO OXFORD STREET

'The starving peasantry of the far West, in the wild outlying
regions of rugged Donegal, possess instinctive skill and artistic
taste that qualify them to produce the textile fabrics for which
Old Ireland was famous.'

The Irish Times, 1887

The rise of the Irish nation is usually traced by rebellions
and risings during the hundreds of years of British control that it
endured, but equally defining was the cataclysmic Great Famine
(1845–1849). The total population was cut by around a quarter; more
than two and a half million people died of hunger and over a million
emigrated. When the immediate danger was past, people were still
at risk, afflicted by malnutrition, typhus and cholera. The population
continued to decline for decades thereafter.

Under the series of laws known as the Penal Code, many Catholics had their lands confiscated and gifted to people with loyalty to the crown but who had no connection to the country. Many were absentee landlords. There had been a profound and long-term neglect to develop industry; the wool trade was long gone and employment in linen had declined due to technological advances. All along the western seaboard, where land was poor and plots were insufficient to support the people, many relied solely on seasonal labouring work or money from emigrated relatives. Weaving and its attendant skills persevered, particularly in the west and northwest of the country, but only on a small scale. This was a very unstable time in Irish history. The struggle to regain lands that had been confiscated and to assert ownership over resources for fishing and farming turned violent. What became known as the Land Wars raged on for decades while pressure for Home Rule mounted. Against this tempestuous and traumatic backdrop weaving emerged as something of a national saviour. It provided employment where there otherwise was none and proved that the innate feel for textiles persisted.

LACE SCHOOLS

Weaving was developed from domestic craft into a viable industry to throw a lifeline to desperately poor communities; it was not the first time that hand skills were used in this way in Ireland. Handmade lace and crochet enterprises emerged from the 1820s onwards as humanitarian responses to poverty and grew in number around the time of the famine. With the exception of the Limerick Lace

GLENGARRIFF TECHNICAL SCHOOLS
IRISH LACE MAKING AND HAND WEAVING
ALL WORK DESIGNED ON THE PREMISES
ORDERS TAKEN   VISITORS ADMITTED

Greeting from Glengarriff

A group of Irish Lace makers of the Lace School Glengarriff Co. Cork. One of the best Lace Schools in Ireland.

The regional styles that evolved in the lace schools remain among the most famous laces in the world: Limerick, Youghal and Carrickmacross.

business established by Charles Walker in 1829, these were run on a non-profit basis, resembling our modern Fair Trade projects.

After their apprenticeships, women and girls could earn as much, and in many cases more, through their lace-making than the men in their families could by labouring on farms. The market for costly handmade lace included royals and aristocrats. The founders came from across the boundaries of religion and class and collectively blazed the trail that others followed, showing that creating luxury goods for a niche market could generate a real income. When weaving was developed after the famine it followed this model to some degree; like lace, it was time-consuming but the outlay for equipment was minimal.

THE WOMEN RISE TO THE OCCASION

Nineteenth-century women who wanted to create change in the world around them had little scope in political life. They could not even vote before 1922 in Ireland, and aside from writing petitions and demonstrating, there were fewer opportunities to impact society on a grassroots level. However, both church and state encouraged women to do good deeds for the poor. At times, the women's motivations included maintaining the status quo, but philanthropy also provided the chance for rare gifted leaders to generate real change. Alice Hart, Lady Ishbel Aberdeen and Agnes Morrogh-Bernard are three who fall into this category.

ALICE HART

Londoner Alice Hart was an artist who had also studied medicine and it is in this context that she first visited Donegal. Already devastated by the Great Famine, the region was experiencing yet more crop failures during the Donegal Famine (1879–1883). Alice's husband Ernest was a surgeon and editor of the *British Medical Journal* and the two travelled together in 1883 to compile a report on conditions. The couple were shocked by what they found in Donegal and touched by the stoic and independent people they met. The Harts responded immediately, using their own money to set up the Donegal Famine Fund to assist the people.

During their visits to Donegal cottages, Hart noticed great hanks of handspun wool hanging from the beams and found many homes alive with the clatter of old looms. Hart was impressed by the standard of the Donegal weavers.

At that time, England was the textile giant of the world. Due to inventions such as the steam engine and improvements in cast-iron technology, the country was the very first to have entire towns dedicated to large-scale factories, and textiles of all sorts were power-loomed in vast quantities. The Arts and Crafts Movement (ACM) was a backlash against this rapid industrialisation. Its founders, William Morris and John Ruskin, sought to counter the devaluing of craft and the erosion of beauty in everyday life and objects, which mass production inevitably entailed. ACM adherents came from the aristocratic and urban, wealthy middle classes. Hart recognised a natural fit; here was the market for Donegal hand weaves.

Hart observed that many of the Irish looms and spinning wheels looked like survivors from the previous century; she was right – some had continued in use since the eighteenth century when they had been distributed in the drive to encourage linen weaving. The Donegal Fund updated looms so that they could weave five and a half times faster. Pattern samples were provided to get the right look for the times. Aniline dyes were in use by then, but Hart knew Donegal Tweed's saleability lay in its contrast to mass-produced textiles, just as handmade Irish lace sold for higher prices than machine-made. Using her scientific background, she experimented systematically with local heathers, lichens and mosses and the Donegal Fund's 'vegetable' dyes won many awards. Hart's Donegal Fund used the outreach model and taught classes in the Irish language, moving experts around the remote little villages to upskill the people.

A TEELIN FARM INTERIOR, CARRICK, DONEGAL, R.W. 1356.

The early woollen industry had been largely destroyed but weaving continued as a domestic craft. It is this that formed the basis of the nineteenth-century Donegal Tweed revival. By the nineteenth century weaving was considered a male occupation, but the important related skills of carding, dyeing and spinning wool were equally relevant. Frequently, the whole family was involved in preparing the yarns and much of the hard work fell to the women.

Wealthy clients were exposed to Irish goods through exhibitions linked to the ACM. In 1886, Hart exhibited Irish lace, Donegal Tweed and her own innovation, Kells Embroidery, in New York. This is perhaps the very first time that Irish tweed crossed over into the American market. The following year, Hart set up a non-profit store called Donegal House close to the upmarket shopping area of Oxford Street in London. Within two years this was expanded to include outlets in Chicago, Philadelphia and San Francisco. The twin benefits of expanding tweed expertise and opening the market were hugely significant for Donegal Tweed in the long term; the benefits are still felt today.

LADY ISHBEL ABERDEEN

Lady Ishbel Aberdeen arrived in Dublin in 1886 as the wife of the Viceroy, the representative of Queen Victoria. From her arrival she threw herself into organising and promoting cottage industry using her influence and unorthodox approach to great effect. Aberdeen arranged a lavish garden party that took place on the grounds of Dublin Castle in March 1886. For the thousand-plus invitees from the leading families, her stipulation was that they all wore dress of Irish manufacture: poplins, laces, tweeds. The event was widely publicised and caused an immediate rush to Dublin shops. At the party, she announced her intention to establish the Irish Industries Association (IIA). The aim was, as she put it:

> 'In order to bring the home cottage, and other industries of Ireland into some sort of working order, and to organise the sale and transition of goods, which however excellent they were, suffered from not being sufficiently known or sufficiently up-to-date in their design.'

Aberdeen's IIA was a very well-organised mechanism; Irish textiles (handmade lace, poplin and luxury tweeds) were honed for the market, then transported to England to be exhibited at events graced by royalty and aristocrats. Irish tweed was a big seller. The proceeds from just one exhibition could yield between £1500 and £2000 (about £150,000 in today's money). Expenses were kept to a minimum so around ninety percent of the takings went directly to the craftspeople.

It is hard to imagine a more ambitious and spectacular celebration of trade, innovation and world culture than the Chicago Fair in 1893. It was spread over almost three square kilometres and featured exhibitors from over forty-six countries. There were two 'Irish Villages' complete with replica castles, stone crosses and thatch cottages. One was organised by Alice Hart's Donegal Fund and the other by Ishbel Aberdeen's

The IIA's Irish Village at the Chicago Fair of 1893.

IIA. Both women brought with them craftspeople who demonstrated their skills of lace-making, weaving, spinning, wood carving and basketry. The fair attracted an astonishing number; over six months, more than twenty-seven million people visited the Chicago Fair.

Ireland was 'packaged' for consumers and tourists alike for the first time. The newly wealthy Irish-Americans responded emotionally; buying Irish-made goods was a way that they could help the people back in the 'old country'. They became an important market for Irish goods. Cutting out the middlemen ensured that the communities benefitted from their work. Aberdeen's village netted tens of thousands of pounds, and with these proceeds from the fair the IIA set up a depot for Irish goods in Chicago. Once the American depots were established, buyers from large stores could easily browse and access Irish goods and this led to the first wave of Irish-interest stores.

Hart was disinclined to join the aristocrats of the powerful IIA and preferred to remain separate, but she and Aberdeen were both openly pro-Home Rule. This was a particularly contentious stance for the wife of the Viceroy. The woman who became president of the IIA after Aberdeen, Teresa Londonderry, was known as 'the queen of

Opposite bottom: Fenwick's was a new upmarket London store which created very costly collections using IIA Irish tweed, some lined with mink, in the late 1800s. The caption on this advertisement reads: 'GOOD NEWS FOR IRELAND … Irish Homespuns are to be the prevailing fashion for Early Spring Coats and Skirts. This delightful change in fashion will be of more practical benefit to Irish peasants than HOME RULE.'

Above: Inspecting bolts of handwoven tweed in County Galway, late 1800s.

Toryism'. Londonderry was known to be a snob and was reviled for her extravagance. Her fine mansion was the centre for deliberations on how to defeat Home Rule. As part of the national movement of rebellion against British rule, the valuable role that Aberdeen played was subsequently largely uncelebrated.

AGNES MORROGH-BERNARD –
THE MOTHER OF FOXFORD

The story of the 'Mother of Foxford' illustrates just how significant the weaving revival was for the post-famine country; it literally built a town.

Foxford, in the northwest county of Mayo, is now a neat and prosperous town, but in the collection of heart-breaking famine narratives Mayo has a high profile. Ruined famine villages still mark the mountainside as ghostly reminders. With absolutely no means to support themselves, the people abandoned villages and poured into the towns in the hope of survival. Once there, they faced unemployment and life in makeshift shacks with no sanitation. As the daughter of a wealthy Anglo-Irish landlord, Agnes Morrogh-Bernard was all set to take her place among her class; her life was mapped out for her, with French finishing school followed by a suitable marriage. She recounted in later life that a pivotal moment came when a desperately hungry woman appeared at her family's home, pleading to be given whatever scraps they were going to throw out or feed to the pigs. Agnes turned her back on her life of privilege, took vows with the Sisters of Charity and dedicated herself to eliminating poverty.

In her new role as head of the convent in Foxford, Mother Morrogh-Bernard recognised that the proceeds of a successful industry could build houses, schools, and the entire infrastructure that the town so desperately needed. The remnants of old mills could be seen lining the fast-flowing river Moy; desperately needed, a large woollen mill could provide everything.

Charles Smith ran Sherrard, Smith & Co., a state-of-the-art woollen mill in Tyrone with an impressive export market. It had forty power looms, machinery for every phase of textile production and combined hydropower and steam with a 'two hundred horse-engine'. Mother Morrogh-Bernard resolved to follow Smith's model. It was an outlandishly ambitious undertaking for a woman in the 1800s.

Providence Mills textiles consignment for the Maharaja of Nawanaga, India.

It is no exaggeration to say that up until the 1980s there was scarcely a home in Ireland without a pure wool Foxford blanket. As a national symbol of luxury and comfort they were customarily given as wedding presents, gifted for new babies and sent abroad to emigrants to remind them of home.

Smith counselled against it, but recognising her determination to proceed, he travelled to Foxford to advise her. Morrogh-Bernard was known to be progressive and non-sectarian in her approach. Despite the fact that she was a Catholic nun and he was a Northern Irish Presbyterian and Freemason, Smith become her firm ally.

The Foxford people responded with enthusiasm; teams of volunteers dug the water channels and helped build their mill. When it was opened in 1892 it was named Providence, which means both 'divine direction' and 'prudent management of resources'. The name became synonymous with quality tweeds and woollen blankets. Every step of the way the profits were put back into the community. From the proceeds of Providence's trade came everything: the housing for the workers, schools, a library, a pharmacy, sports fields, an orchestra, and further education and training for the youth.

ARISTOCRATS AND ROYALS

The contrast between the lives of those who made Irish tweed and those who bought it could not have been starker. In England, the events at which Irish tweed was sold took place in the houses of the wealthy and were part of the social life of the upper classes. These were opportunities to show off and see the latest styles.

For the rising middle class, who aspired to the style of the wealthy, detailed accounts of what lady wore which fabric abounded. When Queen Victoria ordered curtains of Donegal tweed embroidered in Kells embroidery from the Donegal Fund, it was the best advertisement possible.

Just as today, celebratory endorsement fuelled desire. The account of Fingall tweed highlights how this was recognised by those running Irish tweed businesses. Connemara beauty Lady Fingall socialised with the most illustrious Irish people and played tennis with the Duke of York. The Duchess of York admired Lady Fingall's clothes and assumed they were Irish-made. Ashamed to admit they were not, Lady Fingall fibbed. All the women present asked her to get a similar tweed but she had a conundrum; they were German tweeds. She sent a sample cut from her hem to Mother Morrogh-Bernard at Foxford and the tweed was then specially made and delivered within a fortnight. Recognising the opportunity, Mother Morrogh-Bernard asked if this new line might be called Fingall Tweed. Lady Fingall's photograph in the advertisement for 'Fingall Tweed' proved a winner.

Above: Raw wool being distributed to a rural weaver, as it would have been done by the Congested Districts Board.

Below: CDB funded machinery such as these early power looms at Foxford.

Spinning Mills. Convent of Divine Providence, Foxford, Co. Mayo.

THE CONGESTED DISTRICTS BOARD

The country was very politically unstable at the end of the nineteenth century and the conservative Chief Secretary of Ireland, Arthur Balfour, hoped that improving living conditions might reduce political pressure, a policy he described as 'killing home rule with kindness'. His initiative, The Congested Districts Board (CDB), was established in 1891. In this case, the term 'congested' does not mean crowded; rather, it described the situation where the needs of the people exceeded the ability of the land to provide.

The CDB mostly provided vital infrastructure, such as new piers, roads and bridges but also recognised the value of the weaving and knitting trade for poor communities. This government body was hugely significant in the development of Irish tweed. The funding for building mills, buying costly equipment, loans for training and finding markets fell to the CDB. The counties that were the focus of tweed enterprises generally had an existing culture of domestic weaving.

By the nineteenth century Irish weaving had become almost exclusively male; women did the related time-consuming work of carding fleece, spinning yarn and preparing the warp for the loom. The carding, spinning and weaving would take place in the home, and the bolt of tweed would be collected, inspected and finished in a mill. Before the IIA and the CDB, the weavers used to come to places like Kilcar and Ardara on market days and the garment makers would come from the cities to inspect and buy their tweed.

The buyers judged the work based on the absence of flaws in the cloth, the overall design, and the tension in the cloth, and paid accordingly. In this way, those who were talented earned more. The weavers had control over their trade as they could sell directly to the garment makers, but they had the difficulties implicit in transporting their work and working on old equipment. When the CDB set up small factories, which became known as tweed marts, the men could work together to fill orders on quality looms. It was more straightforward to produce tweed to a similar standard in this context. To feed the new weaving enterprises with yarn, the CDB also established spinning mills. The CDB introduced John Kay's invention, the fly shuttle, which made weaving much quicker.

The income generated from woollen mills made a huge impact on rural communities. Wages were very variable in the country. Family income depended on factors such as whether the workers were skilled or could earn in other ways, such as selling chickens and eggs, or by knitting and sewing. As even small children were employed as labourers on farms, their number was also a factor. *Life in the Rosses* (1891) documents a study on labouring families; it estimated that an average family brought home £16 a year (about €1500 in today's money). An account from 1892 by Stratten and Stratten of London shows that the wages Blarney Woollen Mills gave out were equal to the total income of 1250 households:

'Blarney tweeds are unsurpassed by the choicest productions of the Western Highlands of Scotland, and they find equal acceptance in the leading markets of the world, including London, Paris and New York. £20,000 per annum is disbursed in wages alone.'

Chapter Six

THE GAELIC REVIVAL

'Had I the heavens' embroidered cloths,

Enwrought with golden and silver light,

The blue and the dim and the dark cloths

Of night and light and the half-light,

I would spread the cloths under your feet'

William Butler Yeats, 1899

The need to forge an authentic national identity, which Ireland lacked as a quasi-colony of England, became increasingly vital towards the end of the nineteenth century and the start of the twentieth century. But after hundreds of years of English rule and an arts culture that was largely imitative, this was a challenge. What later became known as the Gaelic Revival, also known as the Irish or Celtic Revival, was a diverse effort to find a true Irish voice. It was broad-based and included writers, educators, craftspeople and political leaders.

The spotlight was turned on native ancient culture as a source of

Photo by Anna Frances Levins

Brigit O'Quinn, Banada, Co. Sligo

15th Century Irish Costume

Published by the Gaelic League

A postcard of an event held by the Gaelic League. The events often had a theatrical element and it was customary to don costumes based on ancient Irish dress such as this one. It is made from green tweed, the colour carrying the strongest patriotic resonance.

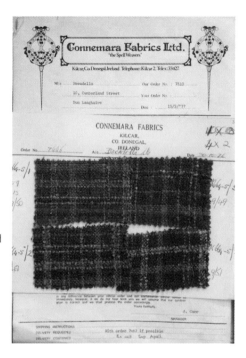

Irish design motifs described Irish identity. Many remained linked with tweed and persisted through the following decades in the form of logos, such as these of the harp and the ancient Tara brooch.

inspiration. Many of the achievements of the Gaelic Revival still shape the country today. Artistically, the elevation of distinctly Irish design elements such as round towers, stone crosses, Celtic motifs, shamrocks and harp symbols arise from this period.

In 1892, Douglas Hyde, who went on to become Ireland's first president, gave a lecture titled 'The Necessity for De-Anglicising Ireland', in which he argued that the country had become a nation of imitators and that pride in language and culture was central to identity. Hyde established the Gaelic League in 1893; it focused on promoting the Irish language and culture. Given the role that manufacturing textiles

Annie Hernon on the Aran Islands, c.1952, creating a colourful woollen belt known as *crios* (pronounced *kriss*) using the islanders' traditional loom-less hand-weaving technique. These belts were wrapped several times around the waist over homespun trousers. Used as belts, ties, and in hats and bags, the traditional crios continues to be a feature of Irish design. Crios such as the ones pictured opposite, handwoven by Liz Christy, also feature in the hand-fastening ritual of Celtic-themed weddings.

had played in Irish life, and the way that it had been controlled and survived against the odds, it was inevitable that wearing Irish-made cloth became a tangible expression of national pride. Irish tweed was subsumed into a broader narrative of patriotism. At Gaelic League events dressing in tweed in shades of green was a feature, as was wearing styles based on descriptions of ancient Irish dress.

The Gaelic Revival was closely aligned to the Irish Literary Revival, of which William Butler Yeats and Lady Gregory were leading voices. They founded the Abbey Theatre in 1904 with their manifesto 'to bring upon the stage the deeper emotions of Ireland'. One of Ireland's most renowned playwrights John Millington Synge was advised by Yeats to turn to the Aran Islands, off the west coast of Ireland, as a source of inspiration. Synge produced a wonderfully detailed report (*The Aran Islands*, 1907) as well as several plays informed by his time on

Inis Meáin (the middle island). He depicted the islanders as the repository of the native folk-spirit that modernity and foreign influence had failed to annihilate. His work celebrated their way of dress, which remained a distinct style – both elegant and functional. At that time, the islanders still wove homespun for their clothes, long after urban mainlanders had turned to shop-bought textiles in modern styles. A sense of pride and independence in wearing homespuns rather than buying imported cloth was grown during this period.

MAKING TRADITION

As in families, traditions provide bonding, allowing one generation to share something with the following. Around the time of the Gaelic Revival the kilt became an Irish tradition. When considering the best garment to be used as an Irish costume, the general consensus was that our own ancient dress of léine was too similar to women's dresses to be suited for the job. The misconception that the ancient Irish wore tweed kilts had begun in the 1860s when historian Eugene O'Curry gave a series of lectures titled 'On the Manners and Customs of the Ancient Irish'. It is now understood that the meaning of *tuartan* and kilt may have become muddled. The original Gaelic *tuartan* (tartan) is found several times in the fifth-century Irish text the *Senchus Mór*, where it is defined as a 'cloth of every colour'. As such, *tuartan* refers to a pattern rather than a garment.

Kilts are an authentic surviving part of the ancient dress of the Highlanders of Scotland; originally they were more voluminous garments. There was a parallel between the ancient Scottish and Irish dress as the custom of their garb did not include trousers. Both peoples were colonised by England. Scots are often termed 'Gaelic cousins across the water' as the two cultures are so deeply connected. The people known to the Romans as 'Scotti' were migrants from 'Dál Riata', present-day Antrim in Ireland, and the Highlanders are largely descended from the Irish Scotti who migrated to Scotland from Ireland between the fourth and fifth centuries. Scots Gaelic and the Irish language are so similar that native speakers can understand one another. The links were strengthened by the practice of seasonal migration to follow fish and labour on farms. The affinity to the Scots was one of the primary reasons why the kilt was mooted as a suitable Irish garment.

Boys in kilts at St Enda's school, Rathfarnham being tutored in gardening, 1909.

The Irish Defence Forces pipe band at the 1916 Centenary parade, O'Connell Street, Dublin, wearing the national kilt (the Saffron kilt), dyed as léine once were, in a nod to ancient Irish dress. The short capes, fastened with a Tara brooch, pay homage to the ancient brat. Sometimes, shamrocks were added to the edge of the kilt, to make it more Irish. The 'wearing of the shamrock' by soldiers was banned in the late 1880s.

Pádraig Pearse was one of the foremost leaders of the 1916 Rising and was executed for his part in it. He was a highly educated man, a barrister, poet, writer and passionate educator. Pearse played a big part in bringing the kilt into Irish tradition. He founded St Enda's, a school in Dublin which was based on what Pearse described as the key characteristics of the ancient Irish system of education: freedom for the individual student and inspirational teaching. The uniform he chose for St Enda's was the kilt. Irish kilts are a solid colour, rather than patterned as the Scottish ones are. The kilt has also made its way into traditional Irish dance.

WAR AND TWEED

Wars were good for the Irish textile business. Tait's Clothing Factory in Limerick produced all the blankets, jackets, trousers, caps, shirts, socks and haversacks needed by the British army for the Crimean War (1853–56) and also for the Confederate Army during the American Civil War (1861–65).

The 1916 Rising was an armed insurrection to establish an Irish Republic. By then, tweed had become interwoven with nationalism to a large degree; everyone was dressed patriotically in green Irish tweed.

Countess Markievicz was a major figure in the Rising. Seven of the leaders of the Rising were executed, but because of her sex her sentence of execution was commuted to imprisonment. She envisioned women as leaders in a free Ireland, saying 'the old idea that a woman can only serve her nation through her home is gone'. Although she never took her seat in Westminster, she became the first woman elected to parliament in 1918. The Rising took place during the First World War (1914–1918), something of a boom time for weaving. Millions of uniforms

Countess Markievicz's outfit for the Rising was described as a soldierly rig-out of dark green tweed breeches (knee-length trousers) black stockings and heavy boots.

were required; even discounting the English troops, the Irish volunteer soldiers, who were of both nationalist and unionist backgrounds, numbered over 200,000 men. All needed kitting out with blankets, woollen uniforms and frieze coats. Despite the hardship of the war, textile manufacturing raised the living standards of many communities.

As the country was edging towards being a full republic, Irish tweed was worn by the most cultured, literary and high-profile leaders in the country. In 1938, the *New York Times* magazine reported: 'People are wondering whether President Hyde will doff his grey homespuns, and his famous tweed cap which he pulls down at a rakish angle when he goes into residence at the Viceregal Lodge.' To wear Irish-manufactured cloth remains a display of patriotism to this day.

The first president of the Irish Republic, Douglas Hyde, in a herringbone tweed coat, with traditional cap.

Chapter Seven

HAND WEAVING STEPS TOWARDS ART

'Irish hands and Irish materials in the making of beautiful things'

Dun Emer Guild manifesto, 1902

The sort of weaving that was done in the country prior to the 1900s had artistry, and beautiful cloth was undoubtedly produced, but it was in the form of metres of cloth rather than one-off or smaller artistic pieces. Weaving in Ireland was to cross over into art with the help of a few significant women.

THE DUN EMER GUILD

The first of these were the women of the Dun Emer Guild (DEG), an arts and crafts co-operative based in Dublin. For much of its past, Ireland's wealth was largely in the hands of the clergy or the Anglo-Irish class who could afford to commission artistic works. While the castles and big houses traditionally had tapestries on their walls,

Dun Emer rug which sold for €10,000 in Whytes auctioneers, Dublin, in 2017.

these were primarily created in the workshops of Belgium and France prior to the Dun Emer Guild. Writer WB Yeats's sisters, Susan 'Lily' and Elizabeth 'Lollie', were talented craftswomen who made a substantial contribution to publishing and art. Evelyn Gleeson moved to Ireland and joined forces with them to found the Dun Emer Guild in 1902. The Guild was run by and employed only women (thirty by 1905). In their weaving workshop the women produced exquisite rugs, cushions, carpets and tapestries developed around traditional Irish symbols and motifs.

THE WYNNE SISTERS AND AVOCA HANDWEAVERS

South of Dublin, in County Wicklow, the three sisters Emily, Winifred and Veronica Wynne pooled their considerable talents to create a very successful weaving mill in order to provide employment for the locals. Avoca mill had been built in 1723 on the banks of the Avoca river

and run as a co-operative, where farmers could grind their grains and produce
textiles for the nearby copper-mining
villages. It had fallen into dereliction,
but with loans from the Congested
District Board the women kitted out
their new business and provided training. Emily was a fine artist
who brought bright colour
to the weaving. Avoca
Handweavers' work repre-
sented a turning point, a
sort of colour revolution. It
was in the days when open-
top cars were common and
their colourful little car rugs
became hot accessories. They
designed fabrics for the
important Italian designer

A 'Century Rug' created
by Avoca to honour their
heritage. It was based on a one-hundred-year-old Avoca rug which was
found in recent times in perfect condition in an attic.

Elsa Schiaparelli, and their weaves were used for a waistcoat for King George VI and baby blankets for Queen Elizabeth II's children. Their pioneering use of colour was all the more remarkable in that they achieved it by experimenting with giant vats in their garden using flowers and roots they grew or gathered from the nearby Wicklow mountains. Their success confounded the assumption of the times that women were unsuited to running businesses.

MURIEL GAHAN

From the 1930s onwards, Muriel Gahan played arguably the biggest role in bringing traditional weaving into a new sphere. One reason why Gahan was so effective was her longevity; she was dedicated to promoting Irish hand skills for over half a century. Gahan's father had worked for the Congested District Board (CDB), and she had accompanied him on visits to the CDB knitting and weaving enterprises in the west of Ireland. She became passionate about supporting rural craft workers and their age-old ways.

Muriel Gahan's Country Shop, established in 1930 near St Stephen's Green in Dublin, remained a much-loved feature of city life for almost fifty years. It provided an outlet for rural craftspeople as well as being an important centre for meetings and gatherings. It was far ahead of its time in many regards. Aside from serving real coffee in the café (an exotic delectation then), it included a gallery where crafts were beautifully displayed. Gahan's genius was to open up the world behind the object. By presenting artisans' names and working methods alongside their work the viewer was encouraged to see craft as art. In the case of weaving, everything from the raw wool that was spun to the environment in which the weavers worked were part of a narrative woven into the cloth itself.

Gahan set up the Country Markets, arranged major exhibitions and hosted competitions to keep standards high. Nine-tenths of the work around weaving was the women's work with the yarn. In a bid to protect it, she set up the Irish Homespun Society (IHS). The IHS organised exhibitions and compiled reports to flag the need for government to fund training and support hand weavers and spinners. Gahan's approach to documenting real craft workers' practices and shaping assistance around this ultimately informed the Crafts Council of Ireland (now the Design and Crafts Council of Ireland). Some of the qualities observable in the Irish craft scene – confidence and a sense of self-worth – are part of Muriel Gahan's legacy.

LILLIAS MITCHELL

The studio craft model became most clearly established by Lillias Mitchell. Mitchell was an award-winning artist from an Anglo-Irish family. She revived and documented the country's vanishing ancient crafts. From 1946, she ran her own weaving workshop and was subsequently asked to set up the weaving department in Dublin's National College of Art and Design (NCAD). When this department opened in 1951 it was the first of its kind. She went on to co-found the Irish Guild of Weavers. The results of Mitchell's work continue to shape the weaving inheritance today as will be seen later in the book.

Traditional hand weaver and spinner working from home on the Aran Islands c.1952. Gahan and Mitchell both researched and documented the craft of spinners and weavers in detail, bringing it to the public's attention and asserting its value as part of the country's heritage.

Chapter Eight

IRISH TWEED –
THE HEADLINE ACT

'Because of the renewed interest in tweed as a fashionable cloth,

sales of Donegal Tweed at home and abroad

have more than doubled.'

The Irish Times, 1955

THE QUIET MAN

John Ford's Academy Award-winning movie *The Quiet Man* (1952) was shot on location in the west of Ireland and was a major hit, grossing $3.8 million in its first year of release. Set against some of the country's most stunning landscapes, it was the most seductive promotion of Ireland possible and a surge of tourism followed its release. The costumes were modelled on authentic clothing and created locally using traditional tailors and Irish tweed. There could be few better ways to show off Irish textile flair.

John Wayne (on the left) during the filming of *The Quiet Man*. Wayne's jacket and trousers were tailored by O'Máille's team using locally sourced Irish tweed. His tweed cap was a variation of the style most commonly worn in Ireland at the time.

The family business O'Máille's Original House of Style in Galway, was at the very centre of this. Stiofán O'Máille co-founded the company with his brother Pádraig in 1938. They had a strong bespoke tailoring side, featuring Donegal Tweed. A number of traditional tailors were employed to make up clothes to their designs. Pádraig and Mary O'Máille were tasked with sourcing the costumes for *The Quiet Man*. After the film, the stars Maureen O'Hara and 'The Duke' (John Wayne) visited O'Máille's shop on Galway's High Street to do their personal shopping. The representation of Ireland's more 'simple' society appealed strongly to Irish-Americans. America's post-war boom meant that more of them could afford to travel. Irish tourism rocketed; the locations where the film was shot became tourist and film-buff destinations; everything pertaining to the Hollywood legends' time in Ireland was of interest. O'Máille's retains its high reputation, stocking natural fibre goods by the finest of the country's artisans.

It was largely due to *The Quiet Man* that the tweed cap became a tourist souvenir. As accessories go, it had already had a very long history. For the vast majority of Irishmen the traditional flat tweed cap was an indispensable accessory for generations. Although most closely associated with the average working man, flat tweed caps were

Contemporary cap in Kerry Woollen Mills tweed created by Hanna Hats.

also worn by the upper classes for leisure activities such as walking and hunting. The tweed cap allowed people to wear high-quality tweed without the outlay of a larger item like a jacket or suit.

Gradually, its use has moved away from being gendered. With the current folk revival and return to heritage and natural fibres, the tweed cap is more popular than ever. Notable Irish headwear makers today include Hatman of Ireland and long-standing family businesses such as Hanna Hats and Jonathan Richards. Most Irish weaving companies make their own lines of headwear which are bestsellers and a great way of showcasing their tweeds.

HAUTE COUTURE

Tweed was traditionally considered a daytime, practical cloth, but in the 1950s it escaped from this confinement. Coco Chanel's tweed suits were soft, and designed to fit more like cardigans than jackets. Inspired by her styles, Irish tweeds began to evolve. Tweed and glamour had not really been connected before, but in the early 1950s, French *Vogue* featured a Dior evening dress made from soft blue-grey tweed, worn with long satin evening gloves. Tweed appeared on Fender guitar amplifiers, in designer furniture, car upholstery – there seemed nothing that could not be improved by it.

In Ireland, the 1950s were an unusual time in that a small group of exceptionally gifted fashion designers were knocking around together; the musical equivalent would be the Greenwich Village folk scene of the 1960s. It resulted in the Irish Haute Couture Group (ICHG), founded in 1962 by Neillí Mulcahy, Irene Gilbert and Ib

The front cover of *Life* magazine (1953)
featured Irish fashion model Ann
Gunning wearing Connolly's Kinsale red
tweed cloak and white Irish crochet-
lace dress with the heading 'Irish Invade
Fashion World'.

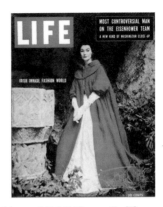

Jorgensen, with members Clodagh Phibbs and Sybil Connolly. These
designers shaped the boutique Irish fashion scene that is such a draw
for buyers today. Each had their distinctive voice and in design terms
all were fluent in Irish textiles.

The arrival of this ebullient wave of talent was at odds with the general atmosphere in the country. Ireland's 1930s' protectionist policy led
to decades of tariffs on imported clothing and textiles, making them
too costly for most people. A tiny minority could afford imported
haute couture or travelled to London and Paris for such style. The
Grafton Academy had been established by the pioneering designer
Pauline Clotworthy in 1938, and talented designers had emerged
from it, but Paris and London swallowed them up. The country
lacked the means or the interest to offer them substantial careers.

Irene Gilbert was arguably the very first to bring Irish design
onto the catwalk when she showed her designs in the upmarket
Dublin city restaurant Jammet's in 1950. Her successful fashion
business provided a model for those who followed. Some of the

wealthiest women in the world, including style icons such as the Countess of Rosse and Princess Grace of Monaco, wore Irish tweed creations by Gilbert.

The 'rag trade' was buoyant in Ireland as businesses focused on goods for export. The designers could draw on the strong network of small garment factories as well as the highly specialised hand skills that proliferated – knitting, embroidery, millinery, crochet, and lace. Some built businesses around imitating styles from abroad.

Entrepreneur Jack Clarke responded to the severe import tariffs by going into production. At one stage, his clothing manufacturing company, Richard Alan, employed more than three hundred staff and was the country's biggest clothing exporter. Clarke was important in growing the Irish fashion scene as he was the first to employ designers for his own collection Country Life.

Sybil Connolly, Ireland's best-known designer from this period, started her career by working for Jack Clarke. Connolly created the romantic styles that captured the imagination of wealthy urban Americans. Carmel White, the editor-in-chief of the American edition of *Harper's Bazaar*, chose a lavish candlelit event in the stunning twelfth-century Dunsany Castle, in County Meath, hosted by Lady Dunsany, to showcase Connolly's work in 1952. Her first collection included an early bohemian take on the traditional red tweed skirts which were still being worn in parts of Connemara.

'Mullaghattan', one of Neillí Mulcahy's designs in purple Donegal Tweed, c.1960.

In the 1960s and early 1970s Ireland's national airline Aer Lingus was an icon of a new and modern Ireland, a model for other newly independent nations. The flight staff were the epitome of style. Donegal Tweed was the chosen fabric and this tradition endured for many years.

The American market has always been important for Irish goods, not only because of the historical connection, but also because America had relatively little manufacturing; its economy was accustomed to importing.

Grafton Academy graduate and Irish Haute Couture Group co-founder, Neillí Mulcahy was admired for her way with tweeds of all weights. Mulcahy had real prowess in tailoring, and an instinctive feel for textiles, something she summed up when she commented, 'The cloth always dictated the design.' In 1963 Neillí Mulcahy got the prestigious commission of designing the Aer Lingus uniforms.

The interest in tweed spurred the development of many new weaving businesses. McNutt of Donegal was a weaving company established in 1953 by William McNutt. It hit the ground running as it got the commission to create the bespoke blue and green tweed for the Aer Lingus uniforms. This period was a turning point. Confidence grew among the makers as they collaborated with designers in the synergistic process of building new, exuberantly coloured and textured tweeds. Suddenly, there was a renewed sense of pride in tweed.

The McNutt weaving team in the 1950s with founder William McNutt on the right. The younger men were trained by older, experienced hand weavers from Ardara, Donegal.

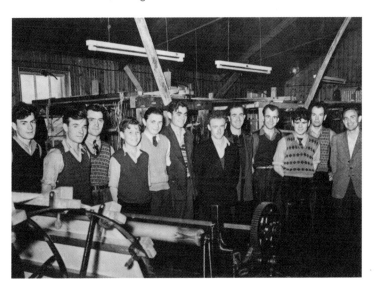

Chapter Nine

THE CALL OF IRISH TWEED

'My father wove mother's sun-lit hues

blanketed fibres, rural colour-infused;

design-dazzled the dull and frugal 'fifties,

exported handweaves to European cities;

those pilgrims bravely, brightly fought,

their carefully crafted cloth eagerly sought.'

Extract from 'The Weaver at Work' by Louis Hemmings

O ver the years many weavers have chosen to settle in Ireland, attracted by the weaving culture. This was the continuation of a long tradition; over the centuries the country had experienced waves of settlers, many of whom stayed, integrated and enriched Irish society.

DONEGAL DESIGN

Alan Hemmings, an award-winning English textile designer, left London to hitch-hike around Ireland, exploring the weaving scene with his young wife Joy. Canon Molloy, a local priest and founder member of The Donegal Historical Society, recognised their potential to create a business for the area. He offered to find them a cottage and gave them a five-year, interest-free loan to set up Donegal Design. The husband and wife team relocated to a rustic cottage with neither electricity nor running water. They were pioneers; in the early 1950s urbanites living 'off-the-grid' was anything but commonplace. They designed and wove unique textiles in bouclés, mohair, and fine new wool while raising their young family under very challenging circumstances. Alan Hemmings loved the flecks of colour that characterised Donegal Tweed. Magee guided them so that their scarves and stoles could co-ordinate with Magee Donegal Tweeds.

Donegal Design advertisement, c. 1965.

Alan Hemmings with a sample of Donegal Tweed-inspired mohair cloth.

The initial success of Donegal Design was facilitated by Irish designers such as Sybil Connolly, who were causing quite a stir with their collections overseas. Alan says:

'Shortly after her [Sybil Connolly] landing in the United States, we were surprised to receive airmail letters with orders from several famous fashion department stores on Fifth Avenue: Lord & Taylor, Bloomingdales and Abercrombie & Fitch.'

Once established, the award-winning company provided training and employed forty people. Donegal Design was eventually taken over by Michael Walsh who continues the tradition to this day.

MOURNE TEXTILES

Around the same time, the talented Norwegian weaver Gerd Hay-Edie also relocated to Ireland and appreciably deepened the pool of talent. Hay-Edie set up Mourne Textiles in 1949, naming it after the beautiful Mourne Mountains close to her home in Northern Ireland. Hay-Edie imported Norwegian looms and machinery and even had a loom made up by the local coffin maker. The design of the loom

Gerd Hay-Edie's innovative fabrics live on. Seen here is a contemporary ballgown by acclaimed Irish designer Peter O'Brien featuring Edie's 'Mended Tweed' handwoven by Gerd's grandson, Mario Hay-Eadie, of Mourne Textiles.

In an American television special about Monaco, Princess Grace
(former actress Grace Kelly) wore a Balenciaga suit featuring
handwoven Irish tweed, which had been presented to her during a
state visit to Ireland in 1961.

was influenced by looms she had used in the Far East. Her inventive and exciting textiles broke with convention. Today, her grandson Mario heads the design-led hand-weaving company. Some of her original designs are still woven and appeal just as much in contemporary times as they did when they first appeared.

GAELTARRA ÉIREANN

American films and iconic photographs, from James Stewart's suits to Jackie Kennedy's outfits, reveal the pre-eminent role that tweed played throughout the 1940s, 50s and 60s. At the upper end, handwoven textiles were in high demand.

Weaving was considered a very practical option for men in rural areas with high unemployment. Although time-consuming, it could be done through the winter months when there was less work on the farm. It was a good fit with country life. Irish tweed had been supported by government funds from the late-nineteenth century by the Congested District Board and this work was continued by the Irish government after Independence in 1922. Weaving and knitting were already well-established cottage industries when Gaeltarra Éireann was established in 1956. It focused on the Irish-language-speaking areas of the country. Its aim was to provide employment to create sustainable communities. Employing hand weavers was incentivised by government funds for equipment, raw materials, training and marketing. These weavers, who are now known as the 'first-wave' weavers, once numbered tens of thousands throughout Connemara, Kerry and Galway, with the highest proportion being found in Donegal.

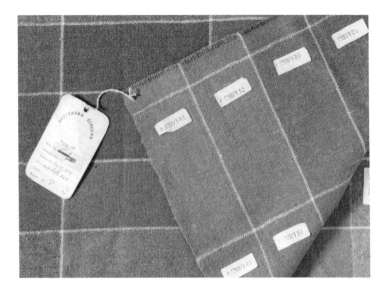

Gaeltarra Éireann tweed samples. Designers were commissioned to keep their tweeds on trend.

GLENCOLUMBKILLE

When Donegal man James McDyer became the parish priest of Glencolumbkille in the 1950s, he recognised that without industry the people would be forced to move to the cities or emigrate. Their Irish-speaking culture, so rich in value, would be lost forever. At that time about one hundred hand weavers in Glencolumbkille worked from their cottages. Every week a van went to the area and when the driver sounded his horn the weavers would come down the side of the mountain, with their bolts of tweed carried by donkeys. The weavers' looms were very basic and consequently they mostly wove *báinín* (the traditional undyed white wool) in quantity. It was then

ASK FOR THEM BY NAME

ROUND TOWER

P   R   O   D   U   C   T   S

Tweeds
Knitwear
Hand-Embroidered Linen

MADE IN THE GAELTACHT — MARKETED BY

GAELTARRA EIREANN

FENIAN STREET & WESTLAND ROW — DUBLIN

An advertisement in *The Bell*, 1947, for Round Tower, a tweed company in Kilkenny which was under government control. The use of Irish symbols, such as the round tower, and the Irish language linked tweed with a sense of identity and patriotism.

dyed different colours and sold for curtains and fabrics.

McDyer was an unusual and driven man, determined to provoke the government into action on behalf of the people. Inspired by socialist structures, he established successful co-operatives. McDyer secured Gaeltarra Éireann funding for updated looms and a weaving factory from which to work. In his autobiography he writes:

> 'The factory was particularly suited to Glencolumbkille because its product, Donegal Tweed, in its various phases, had been a home craft in Glencolumbkille for generations. In December 1954 all this skill was gathered together under one roof to hand-loom the very updated and marketable version of the fabric.'

Even after producing tweed became less of a feature of life for the people of Glencolumbkille, weaving remained at its core. In the early 1990s Taipéis Gael was established. It was a visionary project comprised of a group of young weavers and the older generation who gave their weaving know-how the highly artistic tapestry weaving co-operative.

The American Ambassador, the Irish President Éamon de Valera and Sybil Connolly – who by then had become an ambassador of sorts for Irish textiles – came to open the craft shows in the new community centre. Connolly awarded the trophies for hand weaving and spurred on the revolution in tweed which was taking place due to the efforts of Magee, the designers of Gaeltarra Éireann and talented individuals. In Glencolumbkille Connolly lauded the development of a new lightweight gossamer tweed.

'I myself have seen the women of New York, San Francisco and Sydney applaud loudly at the results of this achievement ... that is in itself an encouragement for us to think up new textures, new weaves, new colours, new designs, in our Irish tweed ...'

Glencolumbkille's tweed trade enabled the workers to renovate their cottages, buy new equipment and contribute to the shared improvements. McDyer described some of the most heartening news of all; two emigrant families returned with their children from England and immediately took employment in the tweed factory.

The contrasting world of the international fashion scene and the rural communities that Irish tweed emerged from is made plain by this image of a model wearing a Sybil Connolly design.

Chapter Ten

CHANGING TIMES

**'There is a certain honesty and authenticity in heritage fabrics
which touch the soul of the wearer ... you feel you're wearing
something that has been handed down from generation to
generation, even if it's been cut in a contemporary design.'**
Designer Clodagh Phibbs, of the Irish Haute Couture Group

I rish tweed always operated in a broad milieu. It could never have
gained the high global profile it currently enjoys if it had not. There
were many important individuals who enhanced its image abroad by
designing in tweed. Government bodies, such as the Wool Secretar-
iat, brought Irish design to shows across the world.

An important player is Jimmy Hourihan, whose coats and capes
became bestsellers in America from the mid-1950s onwards.
Hourihan kept Irish tweed's profile high by selling in upmarket
stores such as Harrods of London and Barneys of New York. The
classic coats from the 1960s and 1970s which he designed now sell

for many times their original value as vintage fashion collectables. Jimmy Hourihan's family business is going strong today producing capes, shawls, throws and coats.

Designers were important for bringing Irish textiles to a larger world over the course of their careers. One of the most famous designers in the world, London-based Irish designer Digby Morton (1906–1983) had many creations in Donegal tweed. Similarly, Irish-based Ib Jorgensen sold his creations in Irish textiles in international designer rooms such as Harrods, Liberty's and Fortnum & Mason.

Clodagh Phibbs created the first truly modern fashion shows in Ireland. Her clothes, under the 'Clodagh of Dublin' label, hit the mark with both Irish women and the export market. The commonality between all of Ireland's leading designers over the decades, however much styles changed, was their profound regard for the country's native textiles. They drew from the rich culture of hand skills, including crochet lace, Irish Aran knit, linen and Irish tweed.

THE PASSING OF THE FIRST WAVE OF WEAVERS

All the time that Irish tweeds were travelling the globe, appearing on fashion show catwalks, or being displayed in the windows of sleek shops in the fashion hubs of Tokyo

Clodagh Design tweed ribbon dress.

and New York, the makers lived in a world apart. To a large degree, government-funded weaving enterprises did what they set out to do, but it was a case of needs must. Spending their days weaving in one of Gaeltarra Éireann's tweed marts was not the life many may have dreamt of as boys. They worked until they could afford to emigrate and create a new life for themselves as far away from looms as possible. In other cases, in order to stay in their own communities, they settled for the work, while the luckier ones discovered a feel and flair for it that made their working life fulfilling.

Power looms did not need rest or food; one could do the job of dozens, and each time they were introduced to an area dozens of hand weavers lost their jobs. But power looms were not the only reason why hand weavers became rarer with every passing decade. In contrast to the weavers of today, who do small runs of highly artistic textiles, weaving acres of tweed was poorly paid, repetitive and back-breaking work. As other opportunities presented themselves, the men deserted the profession.

Ireland changed dramatically from the late 1960s and through the early 1970s. Irish-made tweed clothes were still desired for their quality, and designers carried on working with traditional textiles, but overall, people's ideas around clothing changed. They became less interested in developing relationships with designers and traditional tailors. Penneys (parent company Primark) was established in Dublin in 1969; it offered affordable, street-style clothes. Tourism really took off in the west and there were more opportunities for rural people. Then came the introduction of free university education. This transformed

Irish society over the subsequent years. It led to Ireland's population having one of the highest ratios of further education in the world and more than fifty percent of our people have third-level education today. The following generations became lawyers, accountants and engineers.

DECLINE OF MANUFACTURING

Prior to the 1970s, there had been great scope for important home-grown designers like Pat Crawley, Thomas Wolfangel, Michael Mortell and Richard Lewis to develop collections of a very high standard. This began to change gradually after Ireland voted to join the European Economic Union (EEC) in 1973 and tariffs on imports from low-cost countries were dropped. It led to the first real influx of low-cost clothing into the country. In many cases the styles were more cutting edge than those the Irish companies were making. Almost half of all Irish companies in textiles and clothing were largely or totally dependent on the domestic market. When it collapsed, the cut-and-sew end of the trade was the first to fall. Jack Clarke's business, Richard Alan, once the country's largest clothing exporter, folded in direct response.

The list of council members of the Textile Industry Federation from the mid-1970s makes a funereal read. All over the country, companies that made blankets, linen, cotton, carpets, yarns and textiles closed their doors. Very little effort was made to protect them.

There had been a mill on the Dripsey river in Cork for centuries. The O'Shaughnessy family had established Dripsey Woollen Mills, which became very well known for its tweeds. It closed in the mid-

Blarney Woollen Mills in Cork was given a second chance after it closed in 1973. Christy Kelleher, a former mill worker, bought it, and in a pioneering move created Ireland's largest heritage gift store within the historic mill. This not only preserved the structure but kept its role as a living centre for Blarney. Today, his daughter Freda Hayes is CEO and the company provides a vital outlet for many of the country's best craftspeople.

1970s and today all that remains to tell the story is the silent mill by the river and the 'Model Village' that was built to house the workers.

By the late 1970s a shift had come about; it was agreed that there was a definite place for handwoven goods, but they had to be something machines could not replicate. Weaving had to be driven by imagination.

From the late 1970s, many of Ireland's most important weaving studios have been headed by women, frequently from an artistic background. They have worked towards exhibitions – large-scale collective ventures in high-profile venues. Most hand weavers were solo studio weavers focused on art pieces such as rugs, tapestries or smaller items. Irish weaving heritage had found a home within mainstream art.

Contemporary tapestry weaver Muriel Beckett in her studio in Greystones, County Wicklow. The Scandinavian influence was introduced in the 1950s by Lillias Mitchell and over the following decades it continued to shape Irish weaving. The Irish government funded scholarships for graduates to bring back new skills and Beckett trained in Finland. She discovered an affinity with Finnish aesthetic and working methods, and subsequently shared this with her own weaving students in Dún Laoghaire College of Art and Design.

Concerned that entire skill sets would be lost, those who cared did what they could. Lillias Mitchell continued to play a very important role in preserving and documenting the traditional heritage. In 1975 she founded The Irish Guild of Weavers, Spinners, and Dyers, which replaced the Weavers' Guild. Mitchell's studies were published in *Irish Spinning, Dyeing, and Weaving* (1978) and in *Irish Weaving: Discoveries and Personal Experiences* (1986). The Irish Guild of Weavers, Spinners, and Dyers circulated a typed newsletter and held monthly meetings with a wider educational component. Guild members travelled to distant locations, bringing back a variety of cultural influences. At the same time, the Guild fostered a strong connection with their Irish roots. There was a tremendous interest in the ongoing tradition of weaving in Donegal. Really, for all the seeming contrasts, they were not so different after all, because despite the high profile of the studio weavers, it was very hard to earn a living wage as a weaver of any sort in Ireland. Ann Sutton described hand weaving in *Crafts* (1978): '... the craft which takes the longest time to do and attracts the smallest amount of money when done.' This was to change about three decades later when we entered our current resurgence.

By the early 1980s, over eighty percent of the clothes in Irish shops were imported. The days when Irish tweed was commonplace in mainstream Irish fashion were over after this point. The mill owners who understood that the future lay not in size but in quality were the ones who survived.

Other casualties of the changing times were century-old trades such as drapers and tailors. Ready-to-wear clothing has become our

1970s advertisement for Magee. Magee were the first to see the writing on the wall for made-to-measure suits from traditional tailors and expanded their ranges of medium- to better-end ready-to-wear men's suits.

norm, but once every small town had drapers. Bolts of tweeds were stacked about the shop for customers to browse. Today it is only older men who can recall the initiation ritual of being brought in to be measured for your first suit. It was a mark of the passing of childhood, and resulted in a suit that could be let out as the youth grew and made to last a lifetime. Having a bespoke tailor-made tweed suit is a service which is still available in Ireland, though on a far more limited scale.

Irish tweed makers learnt to operate outside of the extensive infrastructure they had once enjoyed. It involved a whole new skill set. Increasingly bereft of the domestic market, they turned instead to compete with German and Italian tweeds, to vie for a position at the high end of fashion. As early as the 1960s, the global market had been opened up with the help of the Export Board and by the makers themselves. Magees attended trade shows around the world, including trips to Moscow in the 1960s. John Molloy, of John Molloy & Sons Weaving, Donegal, set off for the upmarket textile quarters of Tokyo, Osaka and Nagoya, carrying his sample books of handwoven tweed, to secure orders. It was a very different time; flying was still

Above: Tailors working in the traditional way on the floor in Waterford in 1907, and, bottom left, Robin Johnson and his father Michael, two of the country's last traditional tailors. The trade has passed down through the Johnson family from father to son for over one hundred and fifty years. Visitors to Tullow, in County Carlow, may see them work, seated in the traditional manner in their workshop. President Higgins (2011–) visited Carlow to have suits made by the Johnsons.

prohibitively costly, and cultures were more remote from one another than they seem today. Mill owners went to trade shows in far-flung places and brought visiting foreign buyers to inspect their mills. Japanese buyers have a great regard for authenticity in production and are very attentive to the processes behind textiles. The Japanese luxury market, high-end Irish-interest stores around the world, and the European fashion houses kept Irish looms busy.

Back home, long-established businesses such as Cleo, of Dublin (1936) and O'Máille's – The Original House of Style (1938) continued to play their part. Loyalty may be considered redundant in the ruthless world of global fashion, but it remains a characteristic

The Fogarty family set up Brendella skirts in 1936. Pictured here is Joady Fogarty, grandson of the founder of the family business, with the tailored skirts made up in their own small factory featuring John Hanly & Co tweeds.

of the surviving old family businesses that once were so numerous. For Dubliners, the Nassau Street storefront of Kevin & Howlin is among the longest-standing fixtures in a rapidly changing city. It was established in 1936 and sells everything in tweed: garments, accessories, suits, hats and bags. Noel Kevin has been in the business virtually his whole life and today he runs Kevin & Howlin alongside his daughter Sarah-Jayne. Their tweeds are woven in Donegal homes by Donegal weavers. The shop is a rare surviving link to the disappearing cottage industry.

Kevin & Howlin shop is a tribute to Donegal Tweed.

Chapter Eleven

TWEED – 'THE MOST VALUABLE AND BRILLIANT FACET'

'Everyone looked down on what was "local", and then the Scandinavians and the Germans came and told us "this is fantastic!" and we began to appreciate what we had all along.'

Philip Cushen of Cushendale Woollen Mills, County Kilkenny

KILKENNY DESIGN WORKSHOPS TO THE RESCUE

The self-assurance evident in Irish textiles and fashion today is partly the result of the Kilkenny Design Workshops (KDW). This was the largest government-funded crafts initiative since the nineteenth century Congested Districts Board. Established in 1963 by the visionary William Walsh, KDW's aim was ambitious: to upgrade Irish design. What partly informed the KDW was a rare example of truly progressive thinking. The government body *Córas Tráchtála* (CT), as Enterprise

European master craftspeople in a range of disciplines were invited to set up workshops in the former stables of the magnificent twelfth-century Kilkenny Castle. Wonderful collaborations and exhibitions resulted.

Ireland and the former Irish Trade Board was called then, carried out research to find out how to increase sales and it discovered that when it came to design, the country lagged to an embarrassing degree. CT invited a Scandinavian group to audit Irish design and the 'Scandinavian Report' followed (1963). The report decried the country's lack of respect for its own crafts and criticised how little was done to encourage or stimulate collaboration and innovation. Among the forgettable and the downright ugly, Donegal tweed shone out. It was cited in the report as 'probably the most valuable and brilliant facet of Ireland's textile industry'. While in other areas European designers were brought in, textiles were a little different as there was a high

Gaeltarra Éireann, autumn 1967 fashion show in Dublin. The descriptions reveal how wonderfully colourful the tweed of the time was. From left to right: burnt orange sherbet tweed dress, turquoise and brown Donegal Tweed dress, purple and turquoise Donegal handwoven tweed dress, a child's green-flecked coat, a peach Donegal Tweed coat dress, and a pink and grey striped Donegal fine handwoven tweed.

degree of expertise within the country.

The importance of design became ever-clearer when times were hard. KDW was crucial because those who headed family-run mills did not have the option of simply looking for another job when there was a downturn. Good design, or a change in design, saved them from going under.

Cushendale Woollen Mill faced a crisis and came through because of KDW. Philip Cushen explains:

'In the 1960s we nearly folded. I went to the KDW and said "Can you help us? Do you want us to do some work for you?" and I met Mortimer O'Shea, the head of textiles, and he said "We won't give you work; we will give you new designs." It was around the time of the Mary Quant explosion – magentas, oranges – the Dublin shops that stocked traditional tweeds nearly threw us out! But it worked. We preserved the heritage *and* took a new approach that we probably would never have taken.'

KEEP UP OR FALL AWAY

While countless others never made it through the changing times, two mills discovered how to keep up by adapting. Both are thriving today.

BRANIGAN WEAVERS

The textile industry was traditionally a major employer in Drogheda. John Branigan's maternal family were in the business and he inherited their feel for it. He developed a jacquard weaving business, Branigan Weavers, creating intricately designed bedspreads. For generations it was taken for granted that your bedding needs were met perfectly by the combination of sheets, blankets and bedspreads. In 1960s Ireland these were made by Greenhills in Slane, Foxford Woollen Mills in Mayo and Branigan Weavers. One day in the 1970s, on a trade trip to Frankfurt, Branigan saw a continental innovation: a duvet. He met with two other Irish traders there, the representative from Foxford Woollen Mills and the other from Greenhills. They discussed the duvet. All three agreed that it was a faddish thing; it would never catch on. 'How wrong we were!' he laughs now. Within a short time, bedspreads were passé.

With staff wages to pay and the mill to maintain, the pressure was on to find a solution. Following the advice of the Kilkenny Design Workshops, Branigan sold his jacquard looms, installed new rapier looms and began weaving natural fibre capes and womenswear. He developed a woven textile using knitting yarns, slowing down his machines to accommodate the very softest yarns like alpaca. It was a success. Aside from a scattering of hand weavers, Branigan Weavers is the last weaving company remaining in Drogheda.

BOTANY WEAVERS

In Dublin's ancient textile hub, the Liberties, buildings which had been abuzz with industry for generations were gradually repurposed or demolished to provide housing from the 1950s onwards. Yet one remained and kept going strong: Botany Weavers. The Hackett brothers bought the Botany Weaving Company in 1932 and they became well known for their tweed womenswear garments which were made up in their own factory near the mill. When demand for Botany's garment tweed declined, they secured a commission to produce hardwearing fabrics for official uniforms; then they moved on to furnishing fabrics and finally, airline upholstery. Botany Weavers is currently the world's largest producer of airline interiors. It is notable that the very last weaving enterprise remaining in the country's oldest centre of weaving has the most global profile

On the bolts of fabric in the samples at Botany Weavers, you can read some of the names of the airlines that are Botany's clients: KLM, Etihad, and Egyptian Airlines.

of all the country's weaving enterprises. David Lawson, managing director, explains the palpable sense of continuity at the Cork Street premises: 'When it comes to our weaving, it's evolution not revolution.'

AN EXCEPTION

There were two hand-weaving businesses from the 1970s that played a strong role in reviving and furthering the culture. One of these was Studio Donegal, which is still going strong. The other was The Weavers Shed, run by the talented weaver and designer Noirín Kennedy (later Pye). In 1973, she and her brother John O'Loughlin Kennedy took the bold step of purchasing the thirteenth-century Kilmainham Mill on the outskirts of Dublin city. Set on the river Camac, the mill had

Beautifully coloured tweeds from The Weavers Shed.

a vertical production, which means that everything from opening out a bale of raw wool to the finished fabric was carried out on site. It was the subject of *Woollen Mill*, one of David and Sally Shaw-Smith's 'Hands and Patterns', a beautiful and important series of films about Irish craft. The Weavers Shed was ahead of its time; it merged old skills with a new approach. This diverse yet harmonious group included women from artistic backgrounds, such as Liz Rackard, who threw themselves into the work, learning as they went, and old hands, such as traditional Donegal weavers. Sadly, the business did not survive beyond the 1980s.

Chapter Twelve

RIDING THE WAVES

'I liken it to going surfing. You catch a good wave and you think,

"This is phenomenal!", and then it ends, and you

have to go and catch another wave.'

William McNutt, McNutt of Donegal weaving company

Irish looms had never been busier than in the early 1980s when as assortment of influential designers became obsessed with tweed. Designers like Vivien Westwood, the queen of punk, who has always had a strong preference for natural heritage textiles, led the way. In some cases, almost half of all the Irish tweed being produced was sent straight to the Italian, German and French menswear trade, when companies like Etro and Hugo Boss were using Irish tweeds in phenomenal quantities. Irish tweeds were the top choice for the design houses of Giorgio Armani, Ralph Lauren, and Anne Klein. The highest-paid models in the world were sashaying down cat-walks wearing fabrics from places with quaint names like Nenagh and Graignamanagh. There was also a return to classic suits and this fuelled desire for tweeds of all weights. Additionally, there was a general, though short-lived, turning away from artificial fibres. Altogether this suited Irish tweeds and knits very well.

In remote Downings in County Donegal, an area best known for uninhabited shorelines, there was the unusual sight of exotic-looking fashion designers making their way to McNutt's weaving company. William, the son of the founder of the mill, recalls the times:

'The early to mid-1980s was the period when I started working in the mill. Nearly all the big names in Paris and Milan were using Irish tweed: Kenzo, Vivien Westwood, Cacharel, Missoni, Max Mara – they were all behind Irish tweed at that time. Irish designers such as Mariad Whisker, Louise Kennedy and Patrick Howard were all using Irish tweed. My cousin John McNutt was held in high esteem as a fabric designer. He'd a very good relationship with those people; they came up to Downings to come up with the tweeds for their ranges.'

The demand for tweed was such that virtually every weaving mill in the country was struggling to keep up.

Then the global recession hit. Businesses closed, unemployment soared, and the sad old familiar pattern of emigration returned. Tearful farewells to the youth of the country were met with a sort of dull reckoning that this was the Irish lot. Long-standing businesses were so much a part of the emotional landscape that their loss was like missing teeth in the face of the towns. It became the norm to

In the early 1980s, natural fibre clothing and Irish tweed were very much in style. The singer and composer Johnny Logan enjoyed a stellar profile when he won the Eurovision Song Contest in 1980 and 1987. He is seen here modelling for Dublin menswear store Alias Tom.

outsource production to low-cost countries. For the mills, if there was a lesson to be learnt from this time, it was never to rely on fashion designers. They lost interest in Irish tweed just as the recession kicked in, creating a double-whammy.

Brian Hanly, of John Hanly & Co. tweed-weaving company, also rode the wave of the boom times of the early 1980s. Up to fifty percent of his tweeds went to the Italian, German and French menswear trade. Brian recalls the effect of the recession:

> 'In the latter few years it just fell off a cliff; it was a disaster. I remember it well! If we could have continued to sell enough quantities of fabrics to garment makers, we would have been very happy to just keep creating rolls of fabric, but the whole industry changed.'

The days when designers were on waiting lists for their tweeds were over. It was adapt or die. In response to the fall in demand for tweed from garment makers, mills developed their own ranges. This offered independence and flexibility. Smaller runs allowed them to try things out; if it worked it could be repeated. Mill owners quickly became allergic to what did not sell, a throw lovingly launched mere months ago seemed to gather an odour when met with disinterest in the marketplace. Introducing yarns like silk and linen blends, mohair, alpaca and merino helped them travel further upmarket, where they could enjoy better prices. Some support for small businesses came from government bodies, but ultimately it was up to everyone to try to carve out a niche and stay afloat. It was a time when courage and commitment within the families at the heart of Irish tweed was tested.

After the recession passed, a spectacular boom was generated by a relatively short-lived property bubble between 1992 and the early noughties, which became known as the Celtic Tiger. During the Celtic Tiger years, the country's cash-rich status attracted the

Irish designer Louise Kennedy designed the Aer Lingus uniform featuring Donegal Tweed in the 1990s.

global fashion industry. Its targets, particularly young women, were groomed by sophisticated marketing drives. Shopping malls mushroomed, full of big chain stores selling cheaper-than-ever-before clothes. The trend towards outsourcing accelerated and manufacturing was in freefall. In the fifteen years between 1990 and 2005 manufacturing dropped by a whopping seventy-four percent. In the decade leading up to 2005 the number of people employed in the textile sector was quartered. Within the country visitors were important and overseas upmarket stores in countries like Canada, Germany, Japan and America that stocked authentic Irish tweeds were crucial. But nationally it was a time of indifference to heritage textiles as the country 'lost the run of itself'. Qualities that for so long had sold Irish textiles nationally became progressively less relevant – qualities

Opposite: The award-winning designer John Rocha helped to keep Irish tweed, crochet and knit on the world stage. Pictured here is a John Rocha skirt in a Donegal salt 'n' pepper tweed. As he puts it simply, 'Beautiful *fabrics* last; synthetics don't.'

such as the character of cloth, good design and skilful execution. Irish tweed completed its long goodbye to mainstream fashion.

If it were not for the export market, most tweed makers would not have survived the late 1990s. Fortunately, they did. Once the Celtic Tiger bubble had burst and the country had undergone another economic downturn, appreciation for what had been so very nearly lost surged.

Irish presidents traditionally wear Irish tweed and gift it to visitors. Here, President Mary McAleese (1997–2011) inspects a Guard of Honour at a 1916 Commemoration. President Higgins (2011–) has brought guests to Magee to be fitted out in Donegal Tweed suits.

Chapter Thirteen

DAYS OF RESURGENCE

'Ireland's new tweed designers have a passion for quality, heritage and authenticity. Modern Irish tweed is now all about luxury, beauty and desirability, products designed and made for a lifetime, not for landfill.'

Brian McGee, Market Development Director, Design and Crafts Council of Ireland

Ireland's small but vibrant textile community is experiencing a resurgence. The consensus is that around 2010, the period that coincided with the country coming out of the 2007 downturn, the revival of interest in 'Made in Ireland' textiles was noticeable. This interest has continued to grow and has seen a steady increase in sales.

The majority of Ireland's tweed companies are family businesses. Inevitably they have a longer-term perspective. The cyclical nature of the industry is well understood. They can remember boom days when their parents were turning down orders, employing extra people, and gazing at sales brochures for exciting new equipment. Boom days

The Galway-based slow fashion artisan garment company The Tweed Project creates urban style in traditional textiles such as linen, báinín and Donegal Tweed. They collaborate with the acclaimed tweed company, Molloy & Sons Weaving, Donegal, to create bespoke textiles.

were followed swiftly by lean times when their looms would fall silent and staff might have to be let go. Throughout their working lives they may have experienced ups and downs when flexibility and patience needed to be cultivated. Yet, even the most matter-of-fact among them cannot help but feel optimistic in the present situation.

At the centre of this interest in Irish textiles is an esteem for the way that things are done – our use of natural fibres, those small businesses with a lot of heart, and our slow-made, high-quality goods. The entire process is the antithesis of the ugly excess of mainstream fashion. While the fashion industry has continued to accelerate the pace of change in order to maximise profits, consumers have become more informed. The knowledge that almost eighty percent of all clothing is estimated to be destined for landfill has exposed the wastefulness of crateloads of low-cost clothes bound for our chain stores. Revelations around the environmental destruction caused by parts of the international textile industry has provoked questions around the processes behind goods. The world's dominant textiles are by-products of the petrochemical industry that can take hundreds of years to break down in landfill while leaking microplastics into the ecosystem. Ireland's new tweed designers know that the circular economy is essential to sustaining their way of life in a changing world.

The turn towards natural textiles and ethical, sustainable production is an excellent fit for Ireland. Those who appreciate Irish textiles understand that well-crafted classics will be valued and will stand the test of time. The current resurgence of interest in Irish-made encompasses both the traditional woollen mills and the solo textile artists. It offers everyone a new arena, in which differing working models and artistic responses can feed into one another and create a collective new confidence.

SHARING STORIES

Technology has traditionally been viewed as the enemy of craft. For example, when power looms arrived in Ireland, the culture of hand weaving was threatened. But today, technology is saving craft in multiple ways. The backstory behind textiles – their raw materials, their manufacturing methods, the equipment used to create them, the stories of the makers – is of equal interest to the beauty and appeal of the end product itself. Through the online dissemination of information every aspect of this can be shared. If the colour of wild gorse on the hills outside your home is what inspired a throw, this can be effectively communicated with an online video. Muriel Beckett has been weaving in Ireland since the 1970s. Like many others she knows how hard it was to make a living from weaving in the past, but she is heartened at the changes she has seen since the start of this millennium:

'There is a new wave of weavers; the internet presents so many opportunities to reach out into the world and show what you do. If they can produce well-designed, beautiful products in an efficient professional way, then there is room to create new viable businesses. I'm optimistic for them!'

The industrial realm is normally viewed as being in opposition to the hand-weaving world, but these boundaries are being crossed over. Mayo-based hand weaver Deirdre Duffy launched Wild Cocoon in 2016. Duffy innovated cloth to be woven on power looms by Molloy & Sons, which shared some of the features of her handwoven designs. She explains her philosophy:

'I have the idea that in order to "save" hand weaving we have to push it beyond craft and into a world where it's new and innovative.'

Irish textile artists involved are firmly rooted in their rich weaving culture. A new global fibre art movement has gathered pace. Arranging travelling exhibitions, sharing commonalities and new ideas across the globe; these are made feasible because of social media.

Wild Cocoon textiles echoing the colours of the landscape of the west of Ireland.

For the emergent slow-and-handmade weaving and garment businesses now flourishing in Ireland the internet is their greatest ally. It allows them to promote and sell their work globally without leaving their rural locations. Many traditional techniques and old methodologies are fitting very well within progressive business models. This strengthens and revives the tweed heritage.

DESIGNING IN TWEED

The chance to work with traditional textiles of exceptional character continues to draw designers to Ireland. New responses and dynamic collaborations keep the tradition alive and drive it forward. Irish contemporary designers such as The Tweed Project, Alison Conneely,

Bernie Murphy and Natalie B Coleman place Irish cloth at the centre of their collections. The fashion designers' role in inspiring desire is far more important than might be perceived. It is still widely recognised that Ireland's textile heritage is an essential component of the education of upcoming designers.

Today's textile artists draw from the country's weaving heritage. Terry Dunne's handwoven tapestry 'West Coast Sojourn' features handspun, crottle (lichen) dyed wool such as would have been used for garment fabrics in the past. Terry sees the tweed heritage and the world of textile art as linked: 'As weavers we would have more in common than would separate us; a tapestry is still woven in plain weave, just like tabby weave for tweed; the loom and the weaving processes are much the same. It is simply that as textile artists we have become more creative in how we manipulate the materials and the textures.'

LSAD graduate Hong Zhang's work featuring tweed by John Hanly & Co. of County Tipperary.

In the BA (Hons) Degree in Fashion Design in Limerick School of Art and Design (LSAD) students are encouraged to explore the country's traditional hand skills, such as embroidery and knitting, alongside three-dimensional printing and computerised power looms.

Suzanne Marr is the principal of Dublin's Grafton Academy of Fashion Design. Her mother was Pauline Clotworthy, the pioneering fashion designer who established the academy in 1938. The alumni read like a who's who of Irish fashion design through the generations.

At the core of the academy's teaching is a strong emphasis on tailoring and the use of quality textiles, such as Irish tweed, which designers love to work with because of the way it can be shaped. Marr sees the renewed focus on Irish textiles as part of a sea change:

> 'Generally clothing is more about individual expression now, in contrast to simply aping celebrities, and the upper end of the market tends to identify far more with the ethos of garments … great design is what is central, of course, but if it can be combined with heritage into a creative vision – it will always be a winning combination.'

However beautiful a piece of cloth is, it must be seen *in* something to be fully appreciated. This is why getting designers and tweed companies together is so exhilarating. The Design and Crafts Council of Ireland (DCCoI) is the national agency tasked with supporting small craft enterprises. It encourages collaborations between designers and makers. Their initiative, a boutique trade fair, entitled 'Showcase – Ireland's Creative Expo', features about five hundred exhibitors. While individual consumers might be attracted to the charm of the

DCCoI-supported collaboration: Ringhaddy oak chair by Donna Bates, featuring handwoven tweed from Mourne Textiles, in Newry, County Down.

backstory, international buyers who go to Showcase are looking for more tangible elements: the feel, the look and the durability of traditional textiles. The DCCoI themed fashion shows are a chance to see tweed used in cutting-edge designs and discover the many small textile businesses that are thriving all across the country.

Brian McGee, Marketing Development Director of DCCoI, observes the effect of the resurgence:

'I have always been drawn to the word *Fí*, or *Figh*, which means weave: the act of weaving or something that's woven – textiles, stories and communities – closely knit. Sustainable communities are the anchor of Ireland's tweed-weaving industry. While the 1980s and 1990s saw declines in employment, we are now witnessing a rebirth in rural villages with small, thriving factories with young workers.'

REWARD AT LAST

Solo weavers are well placed to make the most of this resurgence. There were few options in Ardara, County Donegal when Eddie Doherty was a youth in the late 1950s. Doherty left school at sixteen to learn all aspects of the trade. He was not attracted to it particularly, as he explains: 'When I was a young fella, it was emigrate or weave.' He started weaving with many other local men, but most have since emigrated, given up weaving or died. Fortunately, Eddie discovered he had a great talent and passion for his work.

Sixty years later, he is still weaving. The skill level of weavers like him, of which there are a mere handful scattered around the country,

Liz Christy threading the flying shuttle on her loom.

is regarded with awe by others. The speed that he can weave at and his instinctive, unfailing eye for colour are the two characteristics most commented on.

With the current resurgence, Doherty trades on his exceptionalism as one of the last traditional Donegal weavers. For all the seemingly old-fashioned charm of this, the reality is rather more contemporary. He attends trade shows and secures orders from across the globe. In addition, he has his own range of accessories, produces for Magee's handwoven range of suits and garments, and fills orders from exclusive garment and designer furniture makers.

There are just thirty or so other hand weavers in the country with high professional profiles. Collectively they create innovative and unique textiles. They produce one-offs or small runs of bespoke items rather than tweed by the metre, and they frequently draw from the heritage for design inspiration.

Among these is Liz Christy, who has been a professional hand weaver for almost four decades. She remembers in the late 1990s it seemed that her trade had finally been relegated to the margins, becoming perhaps a passionate hobby, like handmade lace, or destined to be reduced to a tourist sideshow. But fortunately the current resurgence proved her fears unfounded. Her hand-weaving business, Swallow Studios, in County Monaghan, is in expansion mode. The growing team of hand weavers there are busy filling orders for her textiles.

CRAFT CULTURE

In tandem with the resurgence of interest in Irish-made and hand-made, the rapid growth of the craft sector since the turn of the millennium has taken many by surprise. The therapeutic benefits of making things with your hands are well known, but the scale, duration and professionalism of this revival suggest that it is far more significant. It is not to be dismissed as too small, hobbyist or too niche; small businesses based on natural textiles are very viable if they are priced correctly. For the first time it seems that weavers can earn a proper living with their hands. It is a fruitful meeting ground between the heritage and the future. The ability to start and sustain small businesses online has led to numerous small-scale initiatives around yarn and hand skills. It is feeding into our tourist market as new festivals pop up and collaborations are everywhere. Workshops for Woollinn, Dublin's indie yarn fest, are booked out months in advance, and dotted around

Craftsperson Sandra Coote spinning fleece from sheep on her farm in County Carlow. The Saxony-style spinning wheel was made by the third-generation spinning wheel maker, Johnny Sheils of County Donegal. It was once the most commonly used style of wheel in the country.

the country are popular wool-related events, such as the Sheep and Wool Museum's All-Ireland wool-spinning championship, Yarnfolk Festival in County Antrim, West Cork Yarn Festival, Woolapalooza in Dublin, and the annual online Tour de Fleece.

Visitors to Clare Island, off the coast of Mayo, can call by the studio of Beth Moran, a textile artist with decades of success running a hand-weaving business. Moran teaches the skills around traditional weaving, including making dyes with natural ingredients from the island's plants. Her nine-month weaver's apprenticeship is always in demand. Beth combines ancient knowledge with the skills needed to set up business in contemporary times, such as how to

'Mick's Rug', seen on Clare Island with Croagh Patrick, Ireland's sacred mountain, on the mainland beyond. The wool used came from Beth Moran's Clare Island herd of black-faced mountain sheep, and is handspun and naturally died with onion skins and lichens before being woven.

communicate your story online. Getting 'hands-on' with wool is one of the very best ways to appreciate Irish heritage, Beth observes: 'Anything that helps people to understand the sort of work that goes into producing textiles is a good thing.'

The spotlight is on our ancient weaving skills. The Irish Guild of Weavers, Spinners, and Dyers reports a downward shift in the age profile of members, as does the Handweavers Guild of Cork. The guilds' calendars brim with members' activities.

A younger generation is bringing weaving, spinning and dyeing out from the margins and away from the threat of extinction. The collective response that the craft revival embodies places Irish textiles where they should be, ready to be developed creatively by following generations.

The Ards Coat with Carnaghan Collar in Donegal Tweed by contemporary textile artist Bernie Murphy.

Chapter Fourteen

LIVING LEGACY

'I'm the sixth generation of weavers in my family. If you just design you don't have a physical thing, maybe you might get it in a few months' time from a factory,

but I can make something, complete it and end up with something that is good to touch, colourful and interesting.'

Kieron Molloy, of Molloy & Sons Weaving, Ardara, Donegal

Although the term 'mill' originally referred specifically to those centres of trade built beside rivers to harness hydropower, today mills are defined more generally as a factory, place or foundry where products are manufactured. Currently, if every surviving Irish woollen mill was amalgamated, it would make just one medium-sized textile factory. But the phrase '*is beag álainn*' or 'small is beautiful' succinctly describes the Irish tweed scene. Irish mills focus on quality above quantity. It would appear that after decades in freefall their number may have finally hit a sustainable level. All Irish-made textiles focus firmly on natural fibres. And the resurgence of interest in Irish-made and natural fibre goods means they are all getting busier.

There are so many ways to let the beauty of tweed into your life. Collectively there is something for everyone: from smaller items such as hats, bags and cushions to suits and coats, throws and rugs. Some mills regard their speciality as homeware while others focus solely on garment textiles. The artistry of the cloth can reveal its origin at first glance. Some are known for their vivid and super-saturated colours; others can be recognised by subtle, natural tones. The patterns, too, are distinctive, created by the weavers themselves or in collaboration with textile designers that work on ranges as part of the mill team. The death of any tradition lies in tired repetition. Ireland's living legacy is vigorous, nourished by the confidence and vision of its makers.

Travelling around the country, every stage of traditional tweed production can still be witnessed. Among the makers, a spirit of collaboration prevails; the overarching importance of preserving the skill set is implicit. It is a surprisingly harmonious realm. *Meitheal* is the name of the old Irish practice of pooling community resources. It is an appropriate simile for the way that the makers interact with one another. When faced with everyday challenges, such as sourcing parts for vintage machines or finishing a run if a machine has broken down, they can turn to one another. It is often personal; those who are in long-standing family businesses feel compelled to honour and preserve it for the next generation. They are sometimes at the very heart of the communities that surround them. Most mills are based in rural areas; local people depend upon them for employment. Mills

Cyndi Graham outside her hand-weaving studio in Donegal. Visitors to Ireland can plot their journeys referencing the Craft Trails that criss-cross the country, stopping off to visit home studios and little mills scattered throughout some of the most unspoilt areas of Ireland.

and the culture of making that they are connected with express the spirit and history of the people. Some Irish woollen mills are situated in historic mill buildings, and although few rely on their mill races, the vestiges of the centuries-old technology can still be seen. The buildings are fascinating examples of early industrial heritage.

Although their number has declined greatly, Donegal still has the highest number of hand weavers in the country. If you visit, you can watch them at their looms, raising and lowering the warp by foot pedals and releasing the shuttle so that it flies across, carrying the weft under and over the warp. The cloth is built incrementally before your eyes. It is said that musicians frequently make the best hand weavers and when you observe the smooth co-ordination of these skilled people this makes perfect sense.

In the past, textile making invariably took place behind closed doors, but as small-scale manufacturing declines, interest in the myriad processes behind it rises. Witnessing textiles being made creates a sense of connection that is a world apart from anonymous mass production. It can be an experience both profound and fulfilling. Castles and abbeys may tell the stories of people's lives and work, but in contrast, woollen mills are a *living* tradition. Because of the personal nature of these visits, they are often cited as the highlight of people's trips.

Weaver and textile designer Anke McKernan at the vintage hand-warping loom in McKernan Woollen Mills, in Tuamgraney, County Clare. Their mill tour combines the modern with the past; visitors can see a state-of-the-art computerised knitting machine in action as well as watching scarves being woven on century-old Hattersley looms.

Visitors to Donegal are struck by its compelling natural beauty, from the drama of its mountains to the vast expanses of pristine shoreline. This is Downings, one of the highlights on Ireland's scenic coastal route the Wild Atlantic Way and home to one of the country's most prestigious traditional textile makers, McNutts of Donegal.

DONEGAL

Donegal people are known for their way with textiles. Their flair for design takes its strength from a background of producing carpets, tweed, linen and knitwear. Donegal is the heartland of Irish tweed. Both newer slow-fashion and well-established businesses rely on the weaving companies there for the quality of their cloth.

What follows is a selection of companies based in Donegal which help to illustrate the wealth of Irish weaving.

DONEGAL YARNS

Nationally there are just three woollen mills producing textiles which spin their own yarns, these are Cushendale, Studio Donegal and Kerry Woollen Mills. In contrast to these three, Donegal Yarns is dedicated solely to producing yarn. It is the largest wool spinner in the country and produces a variety of yarns for weaving, machine knitting and hand-knitting.

As you might expect, considering its name and location, Donegal Yarns is best known for the famous Donegal-Tweed-style yarn. In any one shade there can be up to ten different colours against the base shade, creating the lustre that tweed lovers admire. The ever-changing colour palettes are created by colourist Norah Fadden, a Donegal woman who draws her inspiration from the unspoilt landscapes that surround her workplace. Various collections, using one hundred percent natural fibres, including blends of cashmere, silk

(Left) Wool being wound on to bobbins at Donegal Yarns. (Right) A colour card of yarns spun in Donegal Yarns, showing the typical Donegal Tweed look – nepps (felted wool balls) of contrasting colour against a base tone.

and alpaca, are made and many are bespoke for larger customers such as Magee. Outside of the market of the leading weaving and knitting companies, their yarns are destined for international fashion houses and high-end brands. Manager Chris Wieneger observes:

'Consumers are becoming more aware of their social responsibility about how they purchase clothing. With that in mind, we are developing new products incorporating the origins, heritage and provenance as well as looking at sustainability such as reinstating Irish wool into certain products.'

STUDIO DONEGAL

Studio Donegal in Kilcar, County Donegal is unlike any of the other woollen mills featured as it is the only one which is dedicated exclusively to handwoven Donegal Tweed. It is the closest model to the sort of weaving enterprises that once characterised the area. It consists of a team of hand weavers, a garment-making facility and their own yarn-spinning mill. The mill is set on the same site where a woollen mill has been for almost a hundred years. It was previously Connemara Fabrics, which had phased out hand weaving and moved on to power-looming their tweeds. This move pushed the weaving culture further towards extinction. Realising what could be lost, the company reversed course and reverted to hand weaving in the late 1970s.

Studio Donegal was developed under Kevin Donaghy, who subsequently took it over with his wife, Wendy. They dedicated

Studio Donegal handwoven tweed cushions.

themselves to protecting and furthering authentic Donegal Tweed. They weathered the storms with a creative approach, making small runs of singular cloth. By using their own yarns, they could further differentiate their textures and colour palettes. Today, it is run by Kevin and Wendy's son Tristan, who aims to set the hallmark in hand-woven Donegal Tweed. In contrast to a tourist demonstration, visitors can witness making-in-action in a real working environment. They take their 'Made in Donegal' label seriously – everything is done on site.

MAGEE 1866

Magee 1866 is the largest and best-known Irish tweed company both nationally and globally. It has recently incorporated the date of its establishment into its name. Its founder, John Magee, ran a draper's shop in Donegal town selling handwoven tweeds from the nearby villages. His apprentice, Robert Temple, bought the business in 1900 and ever since then it has been a family business. Over the years the Temples have grown it, firstly from menswear into womenswear, then pioneering more urban, casual styles; all with a high standard of tailoring. Magee has made lines for the likes of Burberry, Hackett, Ede & Ravenscroft, John Lewis and many others. As the principal player in Irish tweed, their fabrics are bought by the top fashion houses and are seldom off the catwalks.

Their flagship garment store is in the centre of Donegal town and just around the corner, set on the banks of the river Eske, is its busy mill. The team produce a range of natural artisan textiles, such as silk and linen mixes, but their primary output remains Donegal tweed.

The company ethos includes a commitment to employing within the country and, to succeed in this, they concentrate on value-added garments. The Temples are well known for their caring relationship with the workers; many in the mill have worked there for their entire adult lives and have other family members in the business too.

In the past, Magee employed several hundred hand weavers who worked within the mill as well as outsourcing to hand weavers. The company still carries a range of handwoven tweeds alongside power-loomed tweeds and these are created by local Donegal weavers. Their finishing facilities are used by other textile makers and are part of the vital textile infrastructure of the country. Magee 1866 is in expansion mode. In 2015 they took over a Scottish mill that was closing and installed eight lorry-loads of machinery from there at

Magee suit. Although there is plenty of choice in colours, the rich, natural tones that echo the Irish landscape remain classic winners in Donegal Tweed.

their Donegal mill. This has improved their finishing facilities, giving a softer, smoother finish to their tweeds than ever before.

McNUTT OF DONEGAL

William McNutt runs the family business McNutt of Donegal, creating the very finest of textiles since its foundation by his father Bill in 1953. The mill is situated in Downings, north Donegal. William's grandmother used to run a little shop by the pier that stocked fishing and nautical equipment for fishermen. She included a selection of Magee tweeds in her stock.

William's father, Bill, saw an opening in the market. After training in textiles, he persuaded three accomplished weavers from Ardara to move up to Downings and they trained staff. In the beginning there were about fifty hand looms; McNutt moved to power looms in the late 1960s. Over the decades countless international designers have flown into the country specifically to travel up to remote Downings and work with McNutt of Donegal. William's cousin John McNutt contributed considerable textile design flair to the business over the years.

William McNutt appreciates the current resurgence, but for him the good times are part of a bigger picture, as he explains:

'The main players will all tell you they're happy with life. They've created new niches for themselves and we're all slowly getting busier. It's textiles; it's never going to be easy, but hey … you could be in a lot worse businesses!'

McNutt of Donegal pure wool wrap.

William and his team of sixteen still create tweed by the metre, but their main focus is luxury wraps, throws and blankets. The yarns that feature are one hundred percent natural, such as merino, alpaca, linen, silk and pure Irish wool. McNutt is one of the few weaving companies that still weave linen cloth.

MOLLOY & SONS WEAVING

The father and son team of Shaun and Kieron Molloy continue their family's tradition of weaving in Ardara, one of Donegal's tweed heartlands. They are currently a team of six – a small outfit with a very high profile. What the Molloys refer to as 'the shed' is their little mill beside their family home. While other mills diversified into creating ranges of goods, the Molloys make only textiles.

Passing the skills on through the generations: Shaun Molloy at work with his son Kieron.

The fact that they could shrink down to a father-and-son team during the lean times gave them the crucial flexibility needed to survive. Their artisan textiles are very highly sought after within the current resurgence and they are growing.

Kieron's father had worked with his father, but it was not a done deal that Kieron would follow suit. He admits that he rebelled against it a

Coat by Natalie B Coleman in a basket weave Donegal Tweed by Molloy & Sons.

bit as a youth; weaving in the shed seemed a punishment of sorts, and though he helped out a lot during holidays and weekends he saw a different life for himself. He studied industrial design and had a very successful career path. Yet, as he matured, he found himself increasingly drawn back towards weaving.

> 'When I got a bit older, I appreciated it more. I could see the possibilities of what it offered. When I came to it, I picked everything up really easily. I had an advantage; it was sort of natural. I think some people are made this way. We like to make.'

Eighty percent of Molloy & Sons tweeds go to international designer menswear and are destined for the top fashion houses of the world. Nevertheless, they like to remain open to collaborations and experimental runs with Irish designers. Kieron is known for his willingness to push the boundaries of what he can get out of their machines, which has led to wonderful bespoke runs.

THE LAST VERTICAL MILLS OF IRELAND

Vertical mills include every sequence which transforms raw wool to finished textile on site. Once numerous, Cushendale and Kerry Woollen Mills are now the last surviving vertical mills in Ireland. They are both based in historical mill buildings that are several hundred years old.

The beautiful medieval town of Graignamanagh in County Kilkenny. The name of the town means 'the monks' village' as it developed around Duiske Abbey, the largest medieval Cistercian monastery in Ireland. The monks established the mills in the thirteenth century and their trade became a tremendous source of wealth. Incredibly, some eight centuries later, the same mill site retains its connection with wool as it is the location of Cushendale Woollen Mills.

CUSHENDALE WOOLLEN MILLS

The weavers at Cushendale Woollen Mills in County Kilkenny are unique in their use of Flemish textile terms such as 'skerin' (warping creel), 'stok' (production cloth length), etc., which indicate a connection with continental weaving going back centuries.

Cushendale Woollen Mills is a family business headed by Philip Cushen. Weaving is part of the family's history and Philip Cushen can trace his connection to the mill, with its output of functional textiles, back through six generations:

'My father, my grandfather, and my great grandfather made everything the local people needed from blankets to knitting yarns and tweeds. My feeling is that it is important that the knowledge of how we make tweed is not lost.'

Philip Cushen's training began in his childhood. Over the years, a body of knowledge accumulated, it includes understanding wool and the chemistry of dyes, spinning technologies, designing textiles, getting the most out of sophisticated machinery and the finishing processes. A myriad of specialisations is collapsed into just one term: 'mill owner'. Understanding wool, an ever-varying raw material, is critical. The Cushens work with a farmer in County Wexford who breeds the Galway sheep, a native, protected breed with a softer handle wool than many other Irish breeds. In the mill, the sweet smell of wool is in the air as bales of Galway wool are opened out and mixed with lambswool for extra softness. The wool is spun into unique yarns to be woven into soft blankets, throws and accessories or tweeds for homeware. Cushendale's yarns are popular for knitters as well as being used in the carpets for Áras an Uachtaráin, the Irish presidential residence and workplace. The mill's water comes from a granite area which, unlike the water from boglands or limestone areas, is very clear and pure. Dyeing is carried out with careful monitoring of effluent to preserve water quality in the river Duiske.

Cushendale's plain weave tweeds are milled, an extended finishing technique for a smoother finish.

Most tweeds are woven using twill and broken twill patterns, but Philip Cushen prefers the smoother look that a plain weave gives his tweeds. The wools are *dyed in the wool*, which means they are dyed before being carded and spun. From a palette of thirteen differently dyed fleeces Philip balances the tones. Using this technique, rather than simply dyeing the yarn a single colour, gives a variety of tone and a glowing quality to the tweed.

KERRY WOOLLEN MILLS

Kerry Woollen Mills is in Killarney, close to the Ring of Kerry, one of our most scenic tourist routes, which spirals around the tallest mountains in the southwest. The mill is located beside the river Gweestin, which has powered the mill throughout its existence. Since it was established in 1760 it has been in the hands of only two families, the Eagers and the Eadies. Andrew Eadie, the great-grandson of the founder, runs the family business. The old mill building tells the story of hundreds of years of working with wool. The mill is an integral part of Andrew Eadie's life story. He grew up running in and out of the historic mill buildings and after school he trained in Galashiels, Scotland as a textile technologist and completed a postgraduate degree in textile design.

'When you grow up handling the wool and cloth, something rubs off – I have been working the business since I was eleven. I am interested in both process and product; I like the aesthetic of it. I always had the *grá* [love] for it. My son now works with me. We'll see if he does too.'

Andrew Eadie recalls his grandfather spinning Donegal-Tweed-style yarns for weavers, a tradition he is proud to continue today. Donegal Tweed is just one of the mill's very wide range of tweeds. Mainstream fashion may have moved to lighter and blander cloth, but Andrew understands the enduring appeal of chunkier weaves with lots of personality. Andrew Eadie's colour expertise with dyes enables him to reference the saturated colours of the mountains of Kerry through his designs. Kerry Woollen Mills' yarn is sold to knitters and woven into their own items such as blankets – a popular export item – and their range of tweed clothes and accessories. Their top-quality tweeds sell in quantity to garment and headwear companies and are shown off to great advantage in their own range of clothes and accessories.

Kerry Woollen Mills waistcoat and throws for Cleo, Dublin. The mill
specialises in complete products. Every step, from design to the dyeing of
the wools, spinning the yarns and weaving and finishing the cloth, is entirely
their own.

AROUND THE COUNTRY

If you zig-zag across the country from the wild North West, to the
sunny South East to the rolling pastures of the Golden Vale you can
visit the following three important Irish weaving companies which
also have outlets selling beautiful Irish tweed and natural fibre goods.

AVOCA

Less than a hundred kilometres from Dublin city is the otherworldly
landscape of the upland national park of the Wicklow Mountains.
There the blanket bogs stretch to the horizon in shades that vary
with the seasons from dark orange-brown to vivid purple. Nearby is
a popular stop-off for visitors: the original mill building of Ireland's
oldest extant mill, Avoca, established in 1723 as a collective to provide grain and textiles for the local copper-mining community.

As mentioned earlier in the book, the Wynne sisters' business,
Avoca Handweavers, was a great success in its day. But by the time
Donald and Hilary Pratt bought Avoca mill in 1974 it had fallen into
disuse. Ultimately, the family business has become one of the country's top retailers. Yet, irrespective of how Avoca expanded over the
decades, the family kept weaving at its heart. They are proud of the
heritage of their historic mill. The Wynnes were acclaimed for their

Avoca's own-designed range of clothing includes a choice of tweeds, such as the blue herringbone of this jacket.

artistry in colour. Today, Avoca's signature look remains clever design with a fresh and bright colour palette.

FOXFORD WOOLLEN MILLS

Foxford Woollen Mills is in County Mayo in the west of Ireland. The mill is a contemporary example of the role that historic mills can play in communities. It is at the heart of the town of Foxford, a vital and living space where people gather in the café and exhibit in the annual craft fair. Additionally, it is an important employer

Foxford Woollen Mills produces a wide range of goods from throws and accessories to bedwear, all in natural fibres. Pictured here is their own range of furniture upholstered with tweed, alongside their cushions and throws.

with a team of approximately eighty people. Mill tours within the nineteenth century mill share the sequences behind their unique fabrics, from the warping of their giant looms to the finishing of pure woollen cloth.

After the death of Mother Morrough-Bernard, the founder of Foxford Woollen Mills, Sister Colette Wills and Sister Noeleen Maguire ran the successful mill business. When the global recession hit, the mills went into receivership in 1987. A young local accountant, Joe Queenan, was tasked with closing the mill gates for the last time. It was very hard to imagine Foxford without its woollen mills. About ninety people faced unemployment. In a small rural town with little industry, this was a devastating blow to the entire community. Following instinct more than reason, Queenan decided to rescue the mill by taking it over. Today, he is proud to continue the legacy of its founder.

'The reason the mill was established was so that, through the dignity of work, local people could have a decent standard of living and give their children an education. We still have a strong sense of place and we are very conscious of our roots. It is important to us to continue the unbroken process of weaving and finishing which has been going since 1892; we feel this adds great value to the Foxford brand.'

JOHN HANLY & CO

Tipperary is a landlocked rural region of farmland, mountains, lakes and rivers. Here, Denis Hanly repurposed an old flour mill for weaving in 1893. It passed from father to son, and today it is run by Brian Hanly, the great-grandson of the founder.

Unusually, the mill relies solely on green energy. Their own hydro-generation plant produces a percentage of their working energy requirements and the remainder is purchased from a nearby hydro-generation company.

A catastrophic fire destroyed much of their machinery in the 1950s, but the looms survived so they were able to continue. Incredibly, a ledger dating from 1894 also survived, a precious piece of history for this family business.

Today, Hanly is a modern small-scale factory with a retail outlet. It employs approximately thirty people. Hanly produces classic garment tweeds, which can be seen in many top designers' collections, both nationally and internationally. Having moved away from primarily producing bolts of cloth, it is their own-designed tweed headwear and garments which are their main sellers. Currently sixty-five percent of their trade goes to Germany, UK, Holland, USA and Japan. The Hanly 'look' is classic country apparel – beautifully designed check and plaids as well as classic plains. They also produce classic Donegal Tweed.

For over a century and a quarter Hanly has been at the centre of Irish textile production. Brian Hanly says:

'The main thing that sustains us is the fact that we can genuinely say: "Made in Ireland" and that brand is very, very strong. We are still perceived as being good at what we do. We are known for it.'

Clothes by Irish designer Mariad Whisker featuring Hanly's plain and herringbone tweed.

A FINAL WORD

'Still the weavers are making our world

Over and under and over again

Goes the weft on the warp of their looms

Our bodies are covered, our shelters made homes

as we travel through time from cradles to tombs

Over and under and over again

making cloth with the wool on their looms'

Extract from 'Unbroken Thread', Vawn Corrigan

Irish tweed is a living thing; a network of relationships, skills and connections that reach around the country like a web. Those with the know-how to make traditional textiles are a tremendous resource in any country. Ireland is the envy of many for whom traditional textiles are a distant memory. As part of Ireland's legacy, their stories and lives of making enrich us all. But it goes beyond simply maintaining tradition; future innovation relies upon their expertise. The strong ground of the past provides a springboard for the future.

There may be no need for Irish tweed to get any bigger, but after having survived into the present by swimming against the current, it remains a fragile heritage. The same pressures that devastated the

Irish textile industry in the 1980s and 1990s remain and the price of natural fibres has risen in the interim. Manufacturing in Ireland is far costlier than in low-wage countries and imported imitations of Irish tweed are more common in the mainstream than the real thing. Other challenges include the breakdown of the European infrastructure for wool.

There is hope in the present resurgence; it has facilitated a broader appreciation of the value of making in modern-day life. This exciting development needs to be nurtured. The Donegal Education and Training Board has created a Donegal Weaving bespoke course and is in the process of setting up a Weaving Traineeship with placements in weaving companies across the county. The aim is to support the preservation of the craft that is such an important part of our heritage.

Irish tweed belongs to the nation and preserving it will require cooperation between a disparate group of Irish people, from administrators, to those who run trade fairs, to fashion critics, salespeople, designers, publishers, educators, parents, environmentalists, artists, craft lovers and patriots – *all* are needed.

Weavers and garment makers talk about the 'character' of cloth as though it were a living thing. If you touch Irish tweed, your fingers will remember it afterwards; it does communicate. The textures are satisfying and exciting. The look of it is rather like a painting of the land done in yarn. For some, images of silvery limestone under the changing Burren skies, or the blueish green Mayo landscape with its dark granite soul, or Donegal's misty mountainsides trimmed in russet heathers and yellow gorse are variously evoked in the colours of tweed. Of course, it remains nothing more than a simple woven woollen cloth. But from the moment you are born until the moment you die there will be cloth around you; knowing a little about Irish tweed might give that truth a greater significance.

Genuine Irish-made Donegal Tweed clothes from Tweed in the Valley.

SELECTED RESOURCES

General Resources

Craft in Ireland (craft trails, studio
   listings, events), *www.craftinireland.com*

Design Ireland (products, events),
   www.designireland.ie

Handweavers Guild of Cork,
   www.handweaversguildcork.ie

Museum of Country Life, County Mayo,
   www.museum.ie

National Folklore Collection, University
   College Dublin, *www.ucd.ie/folklore/en/*

National Irish Visual Arts Library
   (NIVAL), Dublin, *www.nival.ie*

National Museum of Ireland –
   Decorative Arts & History, Dublin,
   www.museum.ie/Decorative-Arts-History

Showcase Ireland (annual trade fair),
   www.showcaseireland.com

The Design & Crafts Council of Ireland
   (DCCoI), *www.dccoi.ie*

The Irish Guild of Weavers, Spinners,
   and Dyers, *www.weavespindye.ie*

'The Way We Wore' (permanent
   exhibition of Irish dress), National
   Museum of Ireland – Decorative Arts
   & History, Collins Barracks, Dublin,
   www.museum.ie/Decorative-Arts-History/
   Exhibitions/Current-Exhibitions

'Weaving in the Liberties' project,
   Dublin City Council, *www.dublincity.ie*,
   and The Yarn School,
   www.theyarnschool.ie

Featured Companies and Designers

*Note: This is a limited selection of companies
and designers that feature in the book
rather than a comprehensive listing. As a
general guide, if origin matters to you, read
labels carefully and ask questions. You will
find that companies that use or make Irish
cloth are proud to do so and will welcome
your interest.*

Alison Conneely, designer,
   www.alisonconneely.com

Avoca, multiple locations, *www.avoca.com*

Bernie Murphy Textile Artist, Porthaw
   Glen Buncrana, County Donegal,
   www.berniemurphy.com

Beth Moran, textile artist and tutor,
   Clare Island, County Mayo,
   www.clareisland.ie/ballytoughey-loom-2

Blarney Woollen Mills, Blarney, County
   Cork, *www.blarney.com*

Botany Weaving, Dublin,
   www.botanyweaving.com

Branigan Weavers, Drogheda,
   www.weaversofireland.com

Brendella Skirts (Irish tweed),
   www.brendellaretail.com

Cleo, Dublin, *www.cleo-ltd.com*

Cushendale Woollen Mills, County
   Kilkenny, *www.cushendale.ie*

Cyndi Graham Handweaving Studio, St
   John's Point, Dunkineely, County Donegal

Donegal Design, Rathnew, County
   Wicklow, *www.donegaldesign.com*

Donegal Yarns, Kilcar, County Donegal,
   www.donegalyarns.com

Eddie Doherty, Ardara, County Donegal, *www.handwoventweed.com*

Foxford Woollen Mills, Foxford, County Mayo, *www.foxfordwoollenmills.com*

Hanna Hats of Donegal Ltd, Donegal town, *www.hannahats.com*

Hatman of Ireland, Colemanstown, County Galway, *www.hatmanofireland.ie*

John Hanly & Co., Nenagh, County Tipperary, *www.johnhanly.com*

Kerry Woollen Mills, Beaufort, Killarney, County Kerry, *www.kerrywoollenmills.ie*

Liz Christy, Swallow Studios, Castleblayney, County Monaghan, *www.lizchristy.com*

Magee 1866, Donegal town, *www.magee1866.com*

McKernan Woollen Mills, Tuamgraney, County Clare, *www.scarves.ie*

McNutt of Donegal, Downings, County Donegal, *www.mcnuttofdonegal.com*

Molloy & Sons Weaving Ltd, Ardara, County Donegal, *www.molloyandsons.com*

Mourne Textiles, County Down, *www.mournetextiles.com*

Muriel Beckett, Greystones, County Wicklow, *www.murielbeckett.ie*

Ó'Máille – The Original House of Style, Galway city, *www.omaille.com*

Studio Donegal, Kilcar, County Donegal, *www.studiodonegal.ie*

Terry Dunne, Duncormick, County Wexford, *www.terrytheweaver.ie*

The Tweed Project, Galway, *www.thetweedproject.com*

Tweed in the Valley, Gorey, County Wexford, *www.tweedinthevalley.com*

Wild Cocoon, Claremorris, County Mayo, *www.wildcocoon.ie*

Selected Bibliography

Anderson, Fiona, *Tweed: Textiles that Changed the World,* Bloomsbury Academic (2016).

Dunlevy, Mairéad, *Dress in Ireland: A History,* The Collins Press Ltd (2000).

Helland, Janice, *British and Irish Home Arts and Industries 1880–1914: Marketing Craft, Making Fashion,* Irish Academic Press (2007).

Hemmings, Alan, *The Friendliness of Total Strangers: A Donegal Adventure* (2013). PDF from *louis@samovarbooks.com*

Hoad, Judith, *This is Donegal Tweed*, Shoestring Publications (1987).

McCrum, Elizabeth, *Fabric and Form: Irish Fashion Since 1950*, Sutton Publishing Ltd (1996).

Mitchell, Geraldine, *Deeds Not Words: The Life and Work of Muriel Gahan* (Town House, 1997).

Mitchell, Lillias, *Irish Spinning, Dyeing and Weaving,* Dundalgan Press (1978).

O'Byrne, Robert, *After a Fashion: A History of the Irish Fashion Industry*, Town House (2000).

O'Kelly, Hilary, *Cleo: Irish Clothes in a Wider World*, Associated Editions (2014).

Rowe, Veronica, interviews from *irishlifeandlore.com*

Shaw-Smith, David, *Traditional Crafts of Ireland*, Thames & Hudson (2003).

Shaw-Smith, David and Sally, *Hands*, documentaries on Irish crafts produced for Irish television (RTÉ) available from *hands.ie*

Sutton, E. Frank, *Weaving: The Irish Inheritance*, Gilbert Dalton Ltd (1980).

PICTURE CREDITS

The author and publisher thank the following for permission to use photographs and illustrative material:

p135 Alias Tom; pp28, 91 (bottom), 174 Avoca Hand Weavers Ltd; p118 Blarney Woollen Mills; 131 Botany Weavers; 71 (bottom) Bridgeman Images; pp83, 149 Liz Christy; p52, Cleo; p172 Cleo and Mike Bunn; p115 Clodagh Design; p166 (bottom) Natalie B Coleman; p137 Aoife Conroy and Louise Kennedy; pp41 (bottom), 151 Sandra Coote; end papers, pp6, 28 (bottom), 28 (bottom) tweed supplied by The Weavers Shed, 29, 30, 32, 37, 69, 73, 74, 81 (both), 119, 124, 138, 170, 185 supplied by Vawn Corrigan; pp18, 22 Cushendale; pp107 (photo Sasko Lazarov/Photocall Ireland; model Sarah Morrissey), 147 (photo Sean & Yvette), 165 (photo Barry McCaul), 177 (photo Sasko Lazarov/Photocall Ireland; model Yomiko Chen) DCCoI; pp40, 50 Annie Dibble; p159 (both) Donegal Yarns; pp25 (both), 145 Terry Dunne; p49 Edinburgh University Library Special Collections (De.3.76, plate 11); p45 Jim Fitzpatrick; pp23, 27 (bottom), 35, 76 (bottom), 175 Foxford Woollen Mills; p156 Cyndi Graham; pp24, 27(top), 97 Hanna Hats; pp105, 106 Louis Hemmings; pp86, 139 Irish Defence Forces; pp64, 71 (top) Irish Historical Picture Company; p128 Irish Photo Archive; p30 jacket supplied courtesy of Sinéad Kane, image by author; p122 Johnson Tailors; pp33, 125 Kevin & Howlin; p168 Kilkenny Tourism; p80 Laurel Cottage Genealogy; p21 Linen Hall Library; pp8, 15, 41 (top), 121, 163 McGee 1866; pp43 (bottom), 157 McKernan Woollen Mills; p103 McNutt of Donegal; p166 (top) Molloy and Sons Weaving Ltd; pp43 (bottom), 152 Beth Moran; p101 Mulcahy family and National Museum of Ireland; p153 Bernie Murphy; pp17, 19, 47, 55, 76 (top), 88, 122-3 National Library of Ireland; p59 BELUM.P414.1936 Machinery of a Bleach Mill, 1783 by William Hincks © National Museums NI, Collection Ulster Museum; pp67, 110 National Museum of Ireland; pp111, 127 Collection National Irish Visual Arts Library (NIVAL), NCAD, Dublin; p132 John O'Loughlin and The Weavers Shed; p96 Ó'Máille, The Original House of Style; p85 Pearse Museum, St Enda's Park; p102 Robert Allen Photography; pp9, 31, 43 (top), 158 Shutterstock; p73 Sisters of Charity; p57 Sotheby's; pp11, 161 Studio Donegal; p91 (top) Trinity College Dublin; p180 Tweed in the Valley; p141 Tweed Project; pp82, 94 Archives of NUI Galway Library; p90 Whyte's Auctioneers; p113 Wikimedia; p144 Wild Cocoon/Julia Dunin Photography; p146 Hong Zhang.

TEXT CREDITS

The author and publisher gratefully acknowledge permission to include the following copyright material:

p104 Extract from 'The Weaver at Work' by Louis Hemmings (*louishemmings.com*).

If any involuntary infringement of copyright has occurred, sincere apologies are offered, and the owners of such copyright are requested to contact the publisher.

ACKNOWLEDGEMENTS

The very best part of writing this book has been the great people I have met through it. A big heartfelt 'Thank you!' goes to everybody who greeted this project with enthusiasm. You gave me your time, shared your stories with me and opened my eyes to a whole new world. The book had to be small; I hope that those who didn't make the final edit will understand.

Those within the tradition were my resources; I turned to them again and again. Thank you all, most particularly William McNutt and Philip Cushen for reading the drafts. Philip's encyclopaedia-like mind became my library. Thank you, Philip. This book will always remind me of your generous spirit and your witty corrections in red font.

Brian McGee, thank you. Your consistent enthusiasm for this work and your willingness to help at every stage has made all the difference.

While finding images to illustrate tweed was fun, getting them in high resolution and cleared for use proved frustrating and tedious. Luckily, I had Tom Canning's help with this, as I do in countless other ways; thank you, Tom.

I've never thought myself half as able as my dear friend and mentor Dr Eleanor Flegg seems to think I am; her 'of-course-you-can' put me back on track more times than I can say. Thank you for everything, Eleanor.

I first met fellow-writer Louis Hemmings to hear his wonderful family story but came to value our intermittent coffees together for Louis' ability to inspire me. Writing mostly takes perseverance; that's why encouragement really matters. Thank you friends and family, especially my beloved mom, Barbara, for understanding.

And lastly, but mostly, thank you to Michael O'Brien and everyone at The O'Brien Press, particularly designer Emma Byrne for her magic eye, and my patient editor, Susan Houlden, who understood every single time.